AF413430

one pan feasts

one pan feasts

Easy entertaining for any occasion

Dominic Franks

Cont

ents

Introduction

Where It All Started

Welcome to my second book and the follow-up to *Upside Down Cooking*. When I was thinking about ideas for a second cookbook, I wanted it to be about my love of cooking simple, accessible food. Food that can be shared and enjoyed by everyone, whether they are a first-time cook or confident in the kitchen. I grew up in the '70s and '80s in London in a family where food was the center of every occasion. Mum, along with my grandmas, instilled the art of creating feasts to share with family and friends. We'd indulge, but it was always more about generosity than gluttony.

My parents would often host dinner parties, and this being the height of the '80s, we're talking about professional middle-class hosting. A gin and tonic on arrival, four courses, including cheese, and a different wine for each course, not forgetting the ubiquitous hostess trolley, and Bendicks chocolate mints served with real coffee to finish. All the men wore blazers and the women long, flowing dresses, or later on, sparkly, patterned knitwear with shoulder pads. The fug of Dior's Poison would be almost as overpowering as the intoxicating aromas coming from the kitchen.

As kids, we were allowed to say hello to guests as they arrived, but then had to make ourselves scarce, and would take ourselves off to bed in true Von Trapp family reluctance. I remember sneaking downstairs as each course passed from the kitchen to the dining room, admiring what was about to be served, then I'd listen out for the ooohs and aaahs from the guests. The next morning, I'd slip into the dining room to soak in the leftover atmosphere, the air still heavy with the scent of roasted meats, whisky, and Auntie Fran's Silk Cuts.

As I grew older, Mum would let me serve the guests. A soup course was always tricky, but for the main course, I would start with the side dishes, announcing each one with theatrical flair to squeals of delight from the wives—lapping up the praise as though I had cooked the food.

These memorable dinners may have been when my love for hosting and celebrating began, or it could have been the many Sunday spreads that Mum used to make for parties at our house. Birthdays, anniversaries, and numerous Jewish festivals were all marked by the moving of sofas to be replaced by tables draped with giant bedsheets and then generously dressed with the most incredible plates of food. Mountains of bagels, ribbons of smoked salmon, little glass bowls filled with cream cheese or egg and onion, chopped liver, or taramasalata. Fried fish balls were also popular: little round balls, large flat salmon balls, and gefilte fish with a small slice of carrot on top. And there was always Mum's speciality, quiche. Each event was a feast for the eyes as well as the belly.

My Love of One-Pan Feasts

A feast for me is not necessarily a table groaning with food, like some kind of bacchanalian celebration, although it can be exactly that if you so desire. Feasts are about enjoying food in a way that I feel we've lost somewhat in our health- and fitness-obsessed lives. We've forgotten how to enjoy good food for how it tastes and how it satisfies the soul. But, importantly, how to prepare a feast in a way that lets the cook enjoy the party too, and feel the satisfaction of inviting guests to the table and sharing the joy of feasting.

Of course I love nothing more than hosting, but none of us want to deal with the mountains of washing up, stress, and faff that it entails. In my opinion, one-pan feasting is the answer!

There's no better way to celebrate than with a meal made in a single pan—which is why the recipes in this book are made for one pan or sheet, with upside-down creations, and a host of other ways to flip, feast, and enjoy feeding a crowd. I've designed the recipes in this book to make hosting easy, with simple dishes that can be prepared in advance, and served up without a hassle, in a single pan. So you can get ahead for one-pan worknight suppers, weekend feasts, Christmas dinner, and birthday brunches, and take part in the memories created at a dining table when you've lovingly made the meal.

About My Book

I'm hoping that, like me and others across the world, you'll have already embraced the upside-down concept, but just in case you're new to it, let me explain. Upside-down cooking is the simple concept of layering ingredients on a single baking sheet to build a dish in reverse. It's an idea that works brilliantly with one-pan dishes like tarts and pies: start with a drizzle of olive oil, honey, or sugar to help the cooking process, then top the baking sheet with the "filling" ingredients, and complete it with a blanket of puff or shortcrust pastry on top. Once in the oven, the heat from the metal baking sheet below and the cover of the pastry on top, cook the filling to glorious perfection. When baked, you then have the theatrics of flipping the tart or pie over to reveal the finished, glorious dish.

The possibilities are almost endless: from sweet and savory, to one-pan weekday meals and seasonal treats—wherever your imagination and the ingredients in your fridge take you. I often ask guests who are coming to dinner what their favorite meal is, and then turn it into an upside-down version in tart or pie form; taking the essence of the dish and layering it under pastry. I love to take a classic recipe and ponder how it could work in layers, finally adapting it into an upside-down version. Once you have the technique figured out, you can get creative with your own inventions too.

This book is packed full of my favorite one-pan and upside-down dishes for occasions to feast. Some of these moments are classic celebrations, such as Christmas Day, Halloween, or Valentine's Day, while others focus on everyday feasting, like simple, informal dinners to enjoy with friends and family at home. You'll also find a chapter on dinner parties, featuring multiple-course meals to enjoy with guests. There are chapters for all times of the day and occasion, from brunches and picnics to lunches and dinners. There are one-pan dishes for gatherings, large and small, and even mini feasts just for you—a little indulgent treat to spoil yourself. Feel free to follow these recipes to the letter, or use them to inspire your own creations. Whether you embrace the upside down, or simply enjoy the delights of one-pan cooking, I hope you will fill your eyes, hearts, and bellies with the ideas in this book. Happy feasting!

Love, Dom x

Equipment & Ingredients

Simplicity is key when it comes to the way I like to cook, and that extends to the type of kitchen tools and ingredients I use. You're likely to have most of the equipment listed below but I thought I'd share with you some of my most loved and used items, the stuff that works and brings me success. The same goes for basic ingredients; there is nothing fancy here, but they are all essentials when it comes to my style of upside-down cooking.

Baking Sheet

The baking sheet I use is a good-quality jelly roll pan, which measures 15 x 10½ in (38 x 27 cm). It's aluminum, which is a great conductor of heat and perfect for even cooking. It also has shallow sides, making it easier to slide a spatula under the tart, or for putting a board on top for the flip. You don't want to be elbowing the sides of your baking sheet out the way and ruining the shape of the tart, but equally you don't want a flat sheet with the risk of the tart sliding off.

Parchment Paper

I would advise lining your baking sheet with parchment paper, as it prevents the tarts and pies sticking to the baking sheet and allows you to easily flip them over once baked. It also helps to keep the fillings of the larger pies in place, and once flipped over will ensure you can peel off the backing paper to reveal the pie without damaging or losing the top. A small amount of butter around the inside edge of the baking sheet can also help to hold the parchment paper in place.

Egg Wash

I always brush my pastry tarts and pies with beaten egg before they go into the oven. For an egg-free version, you can use a splash of milk or a milk alternative, or even a light vegetable oil. All give a beautifully bronzed pastry after baking.

Food-safe Pencil

For many of the recipes, I suggest tracing around a plate or a template with a pencil. It also helps with knowing where to place the tart topping on the baking sheet if you mark the outline of the tart on the parchment paper first. You should use a food-safe pencil or, failing that, draw on one side of the paper and flip it over, since most parchment paper is transparent.

Oils & Sweeteners

Depending on which recipe you're making, the first ingredient used in all my tarts and pies, sweet or savory, is either olive oil or honey. A drizzle of oil or honey over the parchment paper–lined baking sheet helps cook and add color to your tart or pie, often creating a beautiful golden patina on the top and around the pastry edges. I use a good-quality olive oil for the savory dishes (and sometimes butter). Honey is my preference for the sweet dishes, but this can be substituted for golden syrup, maple syrup, or agave.

Pastry

In the US, ready-made puff pastry and phyllo is fairly common and can be found in the freezer section of most supermarkets. Shortcrust or pie dough can also be found in the refrigerated section of most grocery stores in the US, with one problem—it's round! For many of these recipes, it might be easiest to make your own so you can roll it out to the desired size. Some supermarkets stock vegan and gluten-free versions of premade doughs, which are both perfectly good alternatives.

Pastry Brush

This is a useful tool for brushing the egg wash over the pastry before baking to give it a golden glow. I prefer a silicone brush.

Tape Measure & Templates

For ease and to avoid leftovers, the pastry sheets can be divided into even-sized pieces with some simple math. A tape measure is handy for this, but you can also draw around a baking pan, ramekin, cookie cutter, or bowl for the circular tarts and pies.

Most of the tarts and pies in this book fit into the following sizes (see the table, below) but remember that the pastry can stretch as you handle it, so don't worry if they come out a little misshapen; you can always trim the pastry once it's placed on the baking sheet.

Tart & Pie Dimensions

Premade puff pastry comes in a variety of sizes and sheets per package. In this book, we encourage you to mark the dimensions for the tart in the recipe, then fit it to your sheet. You may have to use more than one sheet, and change the sizes if necessary.

2 rectangles: 6½ x 9 in (17 x 23 cm)	
4 rectangles: 4½ x 6½ in (11 x 17 cm)	
6 squares: 4½ x 4½ in (11 x 11 cm)	
8 rectangles: 4½ x 3½ in (11 x 8.5 cm)	
12 rectangles: 3 x 3½ in (7.5 x 8.5 cm)	

My Go-To Pastry Recipes

If you can't get hold of the right size ready-made pastry easily or just fancy making your own, here are my foolproof recipes that always work for me. The pastry, once made, will keep in the fridge for up to 3 days or the freezer for 3 months, well wrapped.

Simple "Ruff" Puff Pastry
MAKES ROUGHLY A 14 X 9 IN SHEET (500G)

This recipe isn't quite as complicated or lengthy as making "real" puff pastry, but I think it tastes just as delicious and works well with my tarts and pies. There are a few stages to master, but it delivers a wonderfully flaky, layered crust every time. It is inspired by my sister-in-law Mo's recipe, and she makes the best sausage rolls with it. It's definitely a lazy day project. Put the kettle on, do a few jobs around the house, and come back to it every 20 minutes or so and by the end of the day, you'll have a stunning block of pastry ready to use as you wish.

2 cups (250g) all-purpose flour, plus extra for dusting
1 tsp fine sea salt
1 cup (250g) frozen lightly salted butter (place in the freezer 24 hours prior to making), coarsely grated
roughly ⅔ cup (150ml) chilled water

1   Sift the flour and salt into a large bowl. Rub the butter loosely into the flour with your fingertips—you should still be able to see flecks of butter. Make a well in the middle of the flour mixture and pour in about two-thirds of the chilled water, stirring with a clawed hand, until you have a firm, rough dough. Add extra water, if needed, to bring it all together.

2   Flatten the dough out into a rough rectangle, wrap it in plastic wrap and let rest for 20 minutes in the freezer.

3   Turn the dough out onto a lightly floured worktop, knead gently and form it into a smooth rectangle. Using a rolling pin, roll the dough in one direction, until three times the length, about 8 x 20 in (20 x 50 cm), with one of the short sides facing you. It should look marbled with butter.

4   Fold the top third down to the center and the bottom third up, like a letter. Give the dough a quarter turn to the right and roll it out again to three times the length, the same size as before. Fold as before. Wrap the pastry in plastic wrap and freeze for another 20 minutes before repeating this process twice more, turning the pastry a quarter turn to the right each time. The pastry is now ready to use or can be kept in the fridge or stored in the freezer (see above).

Shortcrust Pie Dough
MAKES ROUGHLY A 14 X 9 IN SHEET (400G)

I learned to make pastry from Mum. When I was a kid, I used to spend hours propped up at the kitchen countertop watching her make quiches and tarts, and they all started with a classic shortcrust pastry. Sure, she taught me about measurements and the ratio of fat to flour, but she also taught me not to worry about it all that much. A classic shortcrust is just a combination of three simple, inexpensive ingredients. If you want to throw in ground almonds as well as flour or grated Cheddar cheese instead of some of the butter, then do it. Play with it... what's the worst that can happen? I loved watching Mum bring it all together in a bowl (or even in a food processor, which takes seconds) but most of all, of course, I loved what eventually came out of the oven. After all, anything wrapped in a gloriously golden, melt-in-the-mouth pastry must be good.

2 cups (250g) all-purpose flour
½ cup plus 2 tbsp (150g) cold lightly salted butter, diced
1–2 tbsp chilled water

1 Sift the flour into a large bowl and rub in the butter with your fingertips until you have something resembling breadcrumbs. Keep your movements light and quick. Add 1–2 tablespoons of chilled water and bring it together into a ball of dough with your hands. You may need to add a little more water—the pastry should feel smooth and slightly dry and not too wet, just damp enough to leave the inside of the bowl clean.

2 Flatten the pastry slightly, wrap in plastic wrap and pop it in the fridge for at least 30 minutes. The pastry is now ready to use or can be kept in the fridge or stored in the freezer (see main introduction, left).

Note: Shortcrust or dough for pie crust can also be made in a food processor. Place the flour and butter in first and whizz to the breadcrumb stage, then add the water and whizz again until a smooth ball of dough forms.

Cheese & Herb Shortcrust Pastry
MAKES ABOUT 1LB 5OZ (600G)

This pastry is easy to make and versatile. A sharp Cheddar cheese works well, but you can easily swap it for another type of hard cheese, such as Parmesan, Gruyère, or Red Leicester, each adding its own unique flavor to the pastry. You can also vary the herbs with dried ones working just as well as fresh—simply halve the quantity if using. The pastry can be made by hand, but takes mere seconds in a food processor.

2⅓ cups (300g) all-purpose flour
½ cup plus 2 tbsp (250g) cold lightly salted butter, diced
1¾oz (50g) sharp Cheddar cheese, finely grated
1 tsp chopped thyme leaves
1 tsp chopped rosemary leaves
1 tsp dried oregano
½ tsp mustard powder
roughly 2 tbsp chilled whole milk or water

1 Sift the flour into a large bowl and rub in the butter with your fingertips until you have something resembling breadcrumbs. Stir in the cheese, herbs, and mustard with a fork. Add half of the chilled milk or water and bring it together into a ball of dough with your hands. You may need to add a little more milk or water—the pastry should feel smooth and slightly dry and not too wet, just damp enough to leave the inside of the bowl clean.

2 Flatten the pastry slightly, wrap in plastic wrap, and pop it in the fridge for at least 30 minutes. The pastry is now ready to use, or can be kept in the fridge or stored in the freezer (see main introduction, left).

Sauces & Condiments

These flavorful sauces and condiments add an extra dimension to my upside-down tarts and pies, and while versions of them can be store-bought, it's always nice if you can find the time to prepare your own. They're all easy to make, and once you've tried homemade, it's hard to go back.

Tomato & Olive Sauce
MAKES ROUGHLY 1¼ CUPS (300ML)

½ onion, finely chopped
drizzle of extra-virgin olive oil
2 garlic cloves, finely grated
1 tsp chopped fresh oregano
1 tsp dried oregano
⅓ cup (60g) mixed green and black pitted
    olives, roughly chopped
2 x 14.5 oz (411g) cans chopped tomatoes
1¼ cups (300ml) vegetable stock
2 tbsp balsamic vinegar
1 tsp tomato paste
splash of dry white wine
pinch of sugar
salt and freshly ground black pepper

1   Sauté the onion in a little olive oil in a heavy-based saucepan on medium heat for roughly 6 minutes, until softened. Stir frequently so the onion cooks evenly. Add the garlic and half of the fresh and all of the dried oregano and cook gently for another 4 minutes, or until the onion starts to color. Stir in the chopped olives.

2   Pour in the canned tomatoes, then refill the cans with the stock and add to the pan to remove any tomatoey residue. Stir in the balsamic vinegar, tomato paste, white wine, and sugar, then season well with salt and pepper.

3   Let the sauce come to a boil, then turn the heat down to the lowest setting and let it gently bubble and simmer away for at least 2 hours, until thickened. It should reduce by half, if not more. Stir in the remaining fresh oregano at the end and let cool.

Note: This slow-cooked sauce is my go-to (with and without the olives). It works with many dishes, from dressing a simple bowl of pasta to spooning it on top of a pizza base, and serving it with meatballs. Once made, it can be kept in the fridge for up to 1 week or frozen for up to 1 month.

White / Cheese Sauce
MAKES ROUGHLY 2 CUPS (500ML)

2 cups (500ml) milk (I used skim
    but go with your choice)
⅓ cup (50g) all-purpose flour
3 tbsp (50g) lightly salted butter
salt and freshly ground black pepper

1   Place a saucepan on medium heat, pour in the milk, then add the flour and butter. Using a balloon whisk, gently whisk the sauce for about 6 minutes, until lusciously creamy and thickened.

2   Turn the heat to its lowest setting and cook the sauce for a further 5 minutes, whisking every so often to ensure it doesn't catch on the bottom. Stir in a little salt and pepper to taste. The sauce is now ready to use or turned into a cheese sauce (see below).

Note: This all-in-one method results in a classic white sauce, perfect for lasagna or fish pie, but you can pimp it up by adding your favorite cheeses. For a light, creamy sauce, stir in 3½oz (100g) cream cheese when the white sauce has finished cooking. For a stronger-tasting sauce, add 3oz (85g) grated sharp Cheddar and stir until melted and combined.

Red Onion Jam
MAKES ROUGHLY 3 CUPS (750ML)

3 tbsp olive oil
2¼lb (1kg) red onions, cut in half
   lengthwise, then finely sliced
¾ cup (150g) light brown sugar
⅔ cup (150ml) red wine vinegar
⅓ cup (100ml) red wine
3 tbsp whiskey
2 tbsp balsamic vinegar
salt and freshly ground black pepper

1 Place a large Dutch oven or heavy-based
saucepan on low heat. Add the oil and the
onions and cook gently for 30 minutes,
stirring occasionally, until softened and
starting to caramelize.

2 Add a third of the sugar and cook for another
15 minutes, stirring regularly, then add
the rest of the sugar and the remaining
ingredients. Stir and season with salt and
pepper, to taste. Continue to simmer on
the lowest heat setting until the liquid has
reduced, and the onions are dark and sticky.
It should take 30–45 minutes, depending
on the size of your pan, to become a thick
onion jam.

3 Carefully ladle the jam into sterilized jars
while it's still hot and seal with vinegar-proof
lids. Let the jam cool.

4 Store in a cool, dry place and use within
3 months. Keep in the fridge once opened
and use within 2 weeks.

Pesto
MAKES ROUGHLY 1 CUP (250ML)

⅓ cup (50g) pine nuts
1 bunch of fresh basil, including stalks,
   roughly 4 cups (85g)
½ cup (50g) Parmesan cheese, finely grated
⅔ cup (150ml) extra virgin olive oil
2 garlic cloves, peeled

1 Heat a small skillet over low heat. Add
the pine nuts and toast, shaking the pan
occasionally, until golden. You want to
avoid them burning. Let the nuts cool.

2 Tip the nuts into a food processor with the
basil, Parmesan cheese, oil, and garlic and
blitz until almost smooth. Use right away
or transfer the pesto to a lidded container—
the pesto will keep, covered, for up to 3 days
in the fridge.

Note: You can replace the pine nuts with
pistachios or walnuts. Use arugula instead of basil
for a peppery flavor. A sharp, crumbly Cheddar
cheese also works well in place of the Parmesan.

My No-Knead "Sourdough" Bread

While this bread isn't quick to make, it takes less time than regular sourdough, and tastes similar to the real thing. Rather than the traditional method of kneading the dough on a floured countertop, the dough is stretched and folded while still in the bowl, then let rest overnight for the flavor to develop. The impressive loaf makes a great accompaniment to the dips (see p48) in this book, as well as the main event in the Picnic Loaf (see p71) recipe. You can choose to make one large free-form, crusty loaf or bake it in a loaf pan, or form the dough into rolls for crisp-on-the-outside, soft-on-the-inside buns of joy. The dough can be made a day in advance and then baked in the morning when needed.

INGREDIENTS

4 cups (500g) strong white bread flour
¾ cup (100g) rye or whole-wheat flour
1¾ cups (400ml) lukewarm water
1 packet (7g) instant dried yeast (2¼ tsp)
1 tsp salt (I use a flaky sea salt)
1 tsp extra virgin olive oil, plus extra
    for greasing

YOU WILL NEED

10½ in (26 cm) diameter cast-iron Dutch oven
    or heavy-based ovenproof pot with a lid
stand mixer with a dough hook attachment
    (the dough can be made by hand but it's
    so much easier in a mixer)
large bowl or plastic container with a lid
sharp, serrated scoring knife or blade
    (I use my bread knife)
water spritzer bottle
parchment paper

1. Mixing

Place all the ingredients in the bowl of a stand mixer (or you can mix them by hand in a large bowl) and bring them together into a shaggy mess. This should take roughly 2 minutes. Tip the rough dough into a large, oiled bowl (or large, oiled plastic container with lid). Cover in plastic wrap if using a bowl (or put the lid on) and set aside for 30 minutes. It should be a wettish dough.

2. Stretching & Folding 1

After 30 minutes, liberally oil your hands. While the dough is still in the bowl, stretch and fold it over four times, turning the bowl by a quarter each time. The dough will feel quite stiff the first time you do this, but it will become easier as the gluten relaxes and the dough softens. Cover the bowl with plastic wrap and set aside for another 30 minutes.

3. Stretching & Folding 2

Repeat step 2, above, two more times, stretching and folding the dough, leaving 30 minutes between each set. Each time, the dough will become softer and more pliable, and air bubbles should start to appear—try not to pop them. Repeat for a third time; at this point, I also push my fingers into the dough to create a dimpled effect, which seems to add more air. Cover and let the dough rest in the fridge overnight

(8 hours), if time allows—this will help to intensify the flavor of the loaf. If you are short of time, leave the dough for at least 1 hour, until risen and doubled in size.

4. Set the Oven

After a night in the fridge (or around 1 hour proving), take the dough out of the fridge. Preheat the oven to 475°F (240°C)—this is important, but if your oven doesn't reach such a high temperature, then set it to the highest it will go. It usually takes about 30 minutes to heat up, which is just enough time for shaping and a second prove.

5. Prebaking

To prepare the Dutch oven (or ovenproof pot) for baking, cut a piece of parchment paper larger than the dish, then scrunch it into a ball. Open out the paper and lay it over the top of the dish, ready for the shaped dough.

6. Knock Back the Dough

Oil your work surface and hands, then gently tip the risen dough onto the oiled surface and knock back by gently pressing it into a rough, flattish, oval. (This process deflates the risen dough to remove any large air bubbles and evenly distributes the yeast. It also ensures an even-textured loaf when the dough is left to rise for a second time and finally baked.)

7. Shaping & Second Prove

Take a section of the dough, lift it (stretching it slightly), then fold it over toward the middle of the dough, pressing it down slightly. Continue working your way around the dough; it should start to form a smooth ball with large air bubbles trapped within. Flip the dough over so that the pinched middle is underneath. Using both hands in a cupped shape, work around the dough until it forms a ball; do this two or three times until it forms a perfect round shape. Lift it swiftly but gently onto the parchment paper covering the

dish, which should envelop it slightly as it sinks into the dish. Cover with the lid and set aside for 30 minutes for the second prove.

8. Spritzing, Flouring & Scoring

After 30 minutes, your dough will have risen by about half, and the oven should be at the correct temperature for baking. Spritz the top of the dough with water (or you can add a splash of water and wipe it over with your hand). Dust the top with flour and make a deep, wide slash across the dough using a sharp knife or blade. (I use my serrated bread knife).

9. Baking

Cover with the lid and place the Dutch oven or ovenproof pot in the preheated oven for 25 minutes. Carefully remove the lid and bake for another 20 minutes, until the bread is risen, golden, and crusty. Once baked, carefully remove the bread from the dish—it should sound hollow when tapped underneath if ready. Let the loaf cool completely (or for at least 1 hour) on a wire rack before slicing.

Bru

nch

Brunch must be the best meal of the day, or at least a close contender to Brinner (a combination of breakfast and dinner, and one that should be exclusively eaten in the evening). What I love about brunch is how it feels indulgent—the kind of food you could eat for breakfast, yet probably normally wouldn't. A brunch tends to last longer than either breakfast or even lunch, which lends a fabulous, relaxed air to the proceedings. It's about spending time with a partner and friends, rather than just eating for energy and leaving the table. There are also often cocktails involved, which adds another layer of indulgence and feasting.

Upside Down Croque Madame

As kids, we would go on holiday to Mallorca with my cousins. Like typical young children, we'd expend a lot of energy and suddenly have an insatiable appetite. My mum, or auntie, would give us a small amount of money to go down to the fancy hotel in front of the apartment and order the only food they served at lunchtime: croque madame. It wasn't the best; simply melted cheese between two slices of white bread with ham and egg—but I loved those sandwiches. Here's my upside-down version comprising little squares of cheesy, hammy joy, draped in puff pastry, and baked until seriously golden and crisp, and then finished with a fried egg.

Serves 2

2 premade 9¾ x 10½ in
    sheets of puff pastry or use
    homemade (see p12) rolled
    to 14 x 9 in (35 x 23 cm)
2 tsp Dijon mustard
drizzle of olive oil, plus extra
    for frying eggs
1 tsp thyme leaves
3½oz (100g) sharp Cheddar
    cheese, finely grated
2 shallots, cut into thin rings
6 thin slices of ham
4 square slices of Edam cheese
1 egg, lightly beaten
2 eggs
salt and freshly ground
    black pepper

YOU WILL NEED
large baking sheet, roughly
    15 x 10½ in (38 x 27 cm),
    lined with parchment paper

1   Preheat the oven to 425°F (220°C). Unroll the pastry and cut out two 5½ in (14 cm) squares. Spread 1 teaspoon of mustard over each square, leaving a narrow border around each one. Place in the fridge until needed.

2   Mark out 2 squares on the parchment paper, the same size as the pastry and with space between each one, and place drawn-side down on the baking sheet. Drizzle generously with olive oil and sprinkle with thyme. Season with salt and pepper.

3   Scatter one-third of the grated cheese and a few rings of shallot over the marked squares. Ribbon 3 slices of ham on top of each one, followed by the rest of the grated cheese, divided evenly between the two, and the Edam slices.

4   Lay a square of puff pastry, mustard-side down, over each pile. Using the back of a teaspoon, scallop the edges of the pastry squares to seal. Score the top of each one in a diamond pattern with a sharp knife and then brush with egg.

5   Bake for 25 minutes, until the pastry is golden and crisp. Remove the tarts from the oven and let them sit on the tray for 5 minutes. While the tarts are resting, fry the eggs in a little olive oil in a skillet to your liking.

6   Lay a piece of parchment paper on top of the tarts, followed by a cutting board, and carefully flip them over. Remove the tray and peel off the backing paper. Place the fried eggs on one of the squares and flip the second square on top (cheese-side down) to create a puff-pastry sandwich. Slice diagonally in half to serve.

Coca de Verduras

This traditional Mallorquina "pizza" can be bought in any of the hundreds of *el forns* (bakeries) dotted around the island. While the literal translation of *coca de verduras* is "vegetable cake," it is more commonly known as Mallorcan pizza, and it's so delicious, unbelievably simple to make, and keeps well. I prefer to eat it at room temperature, which means it makes the ideal brunch or picnic dish.

Serves 6

For the coca crust:
2¾ cups (375g) all-purpose flour, plus extra for dusting
1 cup (230ml) olive oil
1 cup (230ml) sparkling water
1 tsp salt, plus extra for seasoning

For the vegetable topping:
1 handful of cherry tomatoes, chopped
½ red bell pepper, seeded and diced
½ onion, diced
½ baby eggplant, diced
½ zucchini, diced
1 garlic clove, grated
1 tbsp sweet smoked paprika
3 tbsp extra virgin olive oil
freshly ground black pepper

YOU WILL NEED
large baking sheet, roughly 15 x 10½ in (38 x 27 cm), lined with parchment paper

1 Preheat the oven to 400°F (200°C). To make the coca crust, place half of the flour into a large bowl. Add the olive oil, sparkling water, and salt, then mix with your hands or a wooden spoon until the dough starts to come together. Add more flour, a little at a time, until the dough is no longer sticky; you may need to add a little more or less than the amount stated. Shape the dough into a smooth ball—it is ready to use right away and there is no need to let it rest.

2 Turn the dough out onto the lined baking sheet and gently press it out into a rough rectangular shape. It should be an even thickness all over, about the same as a regular pizza. Bake the crust for 15 minutes, or until the top starts to turn golden.

3 While the crust is baking, place all the chopped vegetables with the garlic, smoked paprika, and 1 tablespoon of olive oil into a large bowl. Season with salt and pepper and toss together.

4 Remove the crust from the oven when golden. Turn the oven up to 425°F (220°C). Spoon the vegetable mixture on top of the crust, leaving a narrow border around the edge. Pop the coca back into the oven for another 15–20 minutes, until the vegetables are tender and golden in places.

5 Drizzle the top with the remaining 2 tablespoons of extra virgin olive oil and a final generous sprinkling of salt. Traditionally, coca is served cut into squares.

Leek, Corn & Tuna Fritters

I'm regularly asked about living with a vegetarian... how I cope with having to prepare two meals each day, and I often want to give my smart-aleck answer of "like every good housewife, I get up at 3:00 a.m." Usually, I end up telling the truth, which is that I mostly eat vegetarian food myself. On occasion, I prepare what I call a "split dish," where I'll make the base of something that can either have a vegetarian or meat/fish protein added to it at the end. These fritters are a delicious example of this. The key ingredients are mixed in a bowl, then I separate half of it out and mix my half with a can of tuna, and his half with a can of chickpeas. Problem solved.

Makes 6–8

2 tbsp (30g) salted butter, plus extra for frying the fritters
1 tbsp olive oil, plus extra for frying the fritters
1 leek, chopped
4–5 Brussels sprouts, shredded
large handful of chopped herbs (leaves and stalks), such as dill and cilantro
6 tbsp semolina flour (or all-purpose flour)
2 heaping tbsp cottage cheese
2 large eggs
3 tbsp corn (frozen or canned), defrosted or drained as needed
5½oz (150g) canned tuna in olive oil (drained weight)
15oz (425g) can chickpeas, drained
salt and freshly ground black pepper
salad leaves and lemon and lime wedges, to serve

1 Heat the butter and oil in a large sauté pan on medium heat. Add the leek and sprouts and sauté, stirring occasionally, for 8 minutes, until tender. Set aside to cool slightly.

2 Tip the sautéed vegetables into a large bowl, add the herbs and season with plenty of salt and pepper. Stir in 2 heaping tablespoons of the flour, the cottage cheese, eggs, and the corn until combined.

3 Spoon half of the mixture into a second bowl. To one bowl, add the tuna and to the other, add two-thirds of the chickpeas (the remaining third can go into the bowl with the tuna, if you like).

4 Mash the chickpeas with the back of a fork and combine with the rest of the ingredients in the bowl—you may need to add another tablespoon of flour to each bowl to allow everything to come together.

5 Take one of the bowls and form the mixture into 3–4 patties with your hands. Repeat with the mixture in the second bowl.

6 Heat extra butter and oil in a large sauté or skillet over medium heat. Add the fritters and cook in two batches for 4 minutes on each side until set and golden. Place the cooked fritters in a warm oven until you're ready to serve. (Any leftovers will keep in the fridge for 3 days, or let cool and freeze for up to 3 months.)

7 Serve the fritters on a bed of salad leaves with lemon and lime wedges for squeezing over.

Upside Down Tomato & Pesto Tarts

There's something about the combination of fresh sun-ripened tomatoes with basil pesto that reminds me of summers in the Med. We live off Caprese salads when in Mallorca, and I wanted to capture the fabulous combination of tomato, mozzarella, and basil but in an upside-down tart form.

Serves 3

2 premade 9¾ x 10½ in sheets of puff pastry or use homemade (see p12) rolled to 14 x 9 in (35 x 23 cm)
drizzle of olive oil
drizzle of balsamic vinegar
3 heirloom tomatoes, cut into thick slices (you can use a mix of colors, if liked)
1 egg, lightly beaten
salt and freshly ground black pepper

For the cream cheese pesto:

⅔ cup (80g) pine nuts
1½ cups (30g) basil leaves
2 tbsp olive oil
2½oz (75g) good-quality cream cheese
1 garlic clove, peeled (optional)

YOU WILL NEED

large baking sheet, roughly 15 x 10½ in (38 x 27 cm), lined with parchment paper

1   Preheat the oven to 425°F (220°C). Remove the pastry from the fridge and set aside.

2   Start to make the cream cheese pesto. Toast the pine nuts in a dry skillet over medium heat for roughly 5 minutes, shaking the pan regularly to prevent them from burning, until golden. Tip them into a bowl and set aside to cool.

3   Mark out 3 rectangles on the parchment paper, each roughly 4½ x 3 in (11.5 x 7.5 cm) and leaving space between each one, then place drawn-side down on the baking sheet. Drizzle olive oil all over the lined baking sheet, then add a sprinkling of balsamic vinegar, and season well with salt and pepper.

4   Arrange a third of the sliced tomatoes in a row on one of the marked rectangles, slightly overlapping the slices. Repeat with the remaining sliced tomatoes. Set aside.

5   To finish the pesto, add the pine nuts (reserving a few to garnish), basil, olive oil, cream cheese, and garlic, if using, to a blender. Season with salt and pepper and whizz to a fine paste.

6   Unroll the pastry and divide into three equal rectangles, the same size as those marked on the parchment paper. Slather the cream cheese pesto over the pastry rectangles, leaving a narrow border around each one.

7   Drape a pastry rectangle, pesto-side down, over each row of tomatoes. Using the back of a spoon, scallop the edges of the pastry to seal. Score the top of each puff in a diamond pattern with a sharp knife and then brush with egg.

8   Bake for 25–35 minutes, until the pastry is golden and crisp. Remove the tarts from the oven and let them sit on the baking sheet for 5 minutes. Lay a piece of parchment paper on top, followed by a cutting board and deftly flip the tarts over. Remove the baking sheet and peel off the backing paper. Scatter with the reserved pine nuts to serve.

Asparagus, Pea & Potato Frittata

Before we bought our home in Mallorca, we used to stay in a little six-room hotel in Pollença Old Town. Every morning the whole building would be filled with the aroma of frittata slowly cooking on the stovetop. They would put it out for breakfast, and any leftovers would be left for midday snacks. This frittata is perfect for a brunch as it can be made ahead, and is just as delicious eaten hot or cold. It can be adapted to suit the time of the year, too, by using different types of seasonal vegetables.

Serves 6

⅓ cup (100ml) extra virgin
  olive oil
14oz (400g) potatoes, such as
  Yukon Gold, cut into small,
  even-sized chunks (no need
  to peel, if you prefer)
12 asparagus spears, tips left
  whole and stalks thinly sliced
handful of dill, fronds chopped
handful of thyme, leaves
  chopped
½ cup (100g) frozen peas
8 large eggs
salt and freshly ground
  black pepper
mixed leaf salad, to serve

YOU WILL NEED
10 in (25 cm) nonstick skillet
  with lid

1 Heat the olive oil in the skillet on medium heat, and when it's nice and hot, turn down the heat to the lowest setting. Add the potatoes and cook gently, stirring occasionally, partially covered with the lid, for roughly 15 minutes, until softened and beginning to color. Stir in the asparagus and herbs, then season with salt and pepper. Cover with the lid and allow the vegetables to sweat for another 5 minutes.

2 Carefully tip the potato and asparagus mixture into a colander to drain over a large bowl, then pour the oil back into the skillet. Once drained, put the vegetables in the bowl and stir in the frozen peas.

3 Beat the eggs in a small bowl. Pour them over the vegetables, season with plenty of salt and pepper, and stir until combined. Let sit while you reheat the skillet over low heat.

4 Tip the egg mixture into the skillet, spread out the vegetables so they evenly cover the base, and cook gently for about 5 minutes without doing anything. When the egg starts to set around the edge, use a spatula to shape the frittata into a cushion by gently drawing in the sides and gently tipping the skillet to flood the empty space.

5 When the egg is almost set with a little liquid still visible on the top, take the skillet off the heat and let stand for 4 minutes to cool a little. Place a large dinner plate on top of the skillet and carefully flip the skillet so that the frittata is now on the plate. Slide it back into the skillet to cook the underneath for a few more minutes until it is set and lightly golden. (If you feel the frittata needs it, turn it twice more, cooking each side briefly and pressing the edges to retain the cushion shape.)

6 Let the frittata stand for 10 minutes before serving it cut into wedges. Serve with a mixed leaf salad.

Cheesy Leek & Potato Galette

Looking for a quick meal that's easy to make and doesn't compromise on flavor? A galette is a great choice; it's essentially a rustic pastry pizza, and the choice of toppings is endless. I went for potatoes and leeks because that's what I had in the fridge, but you can get creative with whatever you have to hand. Cheese is involved, because what is life without cheese. I also used my homemade Cheese & Herb Shortcrust Pastry (see p13), but plain premade pastry would be just as good. The galette is perfect warm or made the day before and served at room temperature.

Serves 4–6

1 recipe quantity Cheese & Herb Shortcrust Pastry (see p13) or use premade shortcrust pastry, rolled to 9 x 14 in (35 x 23 cm)

For the filling:
2 tbsp olive oil
2 tbsp (30g) lightly salted butter
5–6 baby new potatoes, cut into ¼ in (5 mm) thick round slices
1 tsp chopped thyme leaves
2 leeks, thinly sliced
5½oz (150g) cream cheese
2½oz (75g) sharp Cheddar, finely grated
flour, for dusting
1 egg, lightly beaten
1 tsp each of sesame seeds and poppy seeds, mixed (or extra grated cheese)
salt and freshly ground black pepper

YOU WILL NEED
large baking sheet, roughly 15 x 10½ in (38 x 27 cm), lined with parchment paper

1 Make the pastry following the instructions on page 13 (it can be made in advance and will keep in the fridge for up to 24 hours or in the freezer for 3 months).

2 To make the filling, heat the olive oil and butter in a large skillet (with a lid) on medium heat. Add the potatoes and stir well to coat them in the buttery oil, then add the thyme, and season with salt and pepper. Sauté the potatoes for 5 minutes, turning them regularly. Turn the heat down to low, cover with the lid and let the potatoes sweat for a further 5 minutes, until just soft. Stir in the leeks and sauté gently, covered, for another 7 minutes, until tender.

3 Take the skillet off the heat, let the potatoes and leeks cool for a minute or two, and then stir in the cream cheese and Cheddar cheese. Set aside to cool completely.

4 Preheat the oven to 400°F (200°C). Dust your work surface with flour and roll out the pastry to a large, rough rectangle, about ⅛ in (3 mm) thick. It's fine if it has craggy edges and isn't perfect; this is the rustic look we're going for. Carefully transfer the pastry to the lined baking sheet—it should slightly overhang the edges.

5 Tip the leek and potato filling into the center of the pastry and spread it out evenly, leaving a 1½ in (4 cm) border. Carefully fold the edge of the pastry over the filling in sections, folding and overlapping it as you work around the galette. Brush the pastry with egg and sprinkle with seeds or more grated cheese.

6 Bake for 30 minutes, or until golden brown and crisp. Remove the galette from the oven and let it sit on the baking sheet for 5 minutes before serving warm. Alternatively, let cool and store in the fridge to eat the next day. Bring back to room temperature before serving.

Upside Down Eggs Benedict Tarts

Eggs Benedict is synonymous with brunch, and I wanted to create an all-in-one, upside-down tart version that replaces the muffin part with puff pastry. It's also easier to make as you can be cooking the trickiest part, the poached eggs, while the pie is in the oven.

Serves 4

2 premade 9¾ x 10½in
   sheets of puff pastry or use
   homemade (see p12) rolled
   to 14 x 9in (35 x 23 cm)
drizzle of olive oil
1 tsp chopped sage leaves
6½ cups (200g) baby spinach,
   roughly chopped
7oz (200g) thinly sliced ham,
   roughly chopped
1 tsp chopped dill fronds
1 egg, lightly beaten
salt and freshly ground
   black pepper

For the hollandaise sauce:
½ cup (115g) unsalted butter,
   cut into pieces
3 large egg yolks
juice of ½ lemon
1 tsp Dijon mustard
pinch of cayenne pepper,
   plus extra to serve (optional)

To serve:
4 eggs, at room temperature,
   for poaching
1 tbsp finely chopped chives

YOU WILL NEED
large baking sheet, roughly
   15 x 10½in (38 x 27 cm),
   lined with parchment paper

1 Preheat the oven to 425°F (220°C). Unroll the pastry and cut it into 4 pieces, each about 4½ x 6½in (11 x 17 cm). Place in the fridge until needed.

2 Mark out 4 rectangles on the parchment paper, the same size as the pastry and with space between each one, and place drawn-side down on the baking sheet. Drizzle generously with olive oil and sprinkle with sage. Season with salt and pepper.

3 Place the spinach and ham in a large bowl along with the dill and a drizzle of olive oil. Season with salt and pepper, and mix well. Leaving a ½in (1 cm) border, spoon the ham and spinach mixture over the marked rectangles. Lay the pastry over the top, then using the back of a teaspoon, scallop the edges of the pastry to seal. Score the top of each tart in a diamond pattern with a sharp knife and then brush with egg. Bake for 25 minutes, until golden and crisp.

4 Meanwhile, make the hollandaise. Melt the butter in a small saucepan. Add the egg yolks, lemon juice, Dijon, cayenne pepper, and a pinch of salt to a blender and blend for 5 seconds, until combined. With the blender running on medium–high, slowly add the hot butter in a steady stream until the mix has emulsified into a smooth sauce. Set aside, covered, to keep warm.

5 Bring a large pan of water to a boil, ready to poach the eggs. When the tarts are ready, remove from the oven and let them sit while you poach the eggs. Crack one of the eggs into a ramekin. When the water in the pan comes to a boil, turn the heat down to medium–low and swirl the water with a spoon. Lower the egg into the water and repeat with three more eggs. Gently poach the eggs for 4 minutes for a medium-set yolk, then lift out with a slotted spoon onto a plate to drain.

6 Lay a piece of parchment paper on top of the tarts, followed by a cutting board and carefully flip them over. Remove the baking sheet and peel off the backing paper. Place the poached eggs on top of the tarts and spoon over the sauce. Top with a sprinkling of cayenne or ground black pepper and the chopped chives.

California Tortilla Bake with Spicy Potatoes

The Fig Tree is a wonderful beachside cafe in Venice, Los Angeles, that holds many wonderful memories for me and my husband, The Viking. The setting is glorious, with views of the Pacific Ocean and all the incredible people passing by. The food at the cafe is that typical LA mix of Californian and Mexican cuisines, and their breakfast potatoes are to die for. I have tried to recreate the essence of my favorite dish here as an easy brunch feast.

Serves 6–8

1 onion, roughly chopped
1 yellow and 1 red bell pepper, seeded and sliced
2 large flat mushrooms, thickly sliced
drizzle of olive oil
2 tbsp chipotle fajita seasoning mix
7oz (200g) thinly sliced ham, chopped (optional)
2 slightly underripe avocados, peeled and cut into chunks
6 medium-sized tortilla wraps
4 tbsp sour cream
3½oz (100g) sharp cheese, grated (I use Cheddar)
salt and freshly ground black pepper

For the spicy potatoes:
4 large Russet potatoes, cut into small cubes (no need to peel)
2 tbsp (30g) salted butter

To serve:
2 large handfuls of cherry tomatoes, cut in half
2 tbsp finely chopped chives
1 lime, cut into quarters

YOU WILL NEED
large ovenproof dish

1 Preheat the oven to 400°F (200°C).

2 Spread the onion, bell peppers, and mushrooms out in a large roasting dish, and drizzle with plenty of olive oil, then sprinkle with half of the chipotle seasoning mix, and plenty of salt and pepper. Mix everything together, coating the vegetables in the seasoned oil, cover with foil and roast in the oven for 20 minutes. Remove the foil and cook for a further 15 minutes, or until the vegetables are soft and beginning to char a little at the edges. Stir in the ham, if using, and avocados. Let cool.

3 To assemble, take a tortilla wrap and spread a healthy spoonful of the sour cream over the top. Spoon one-sixth of the spicy vegetables down the middle and scatter over some of the cheese. Roll up the wrap tightly, then continue until you have made six rolled wraps. Cut the wraps into thirds and stand each one upright in the ovenproof dish. Sprinkle the top with more cheese and bake for 15 minutes, or until the cheese has melted, and the tortillas are heated through and golden.

4 Meanwhile, cook the potatoes in a pan of boiling salted water for 4 minutes, until just tender. Drain well, then return them to the pan and drizzle with olive oil and add the remaining chipotle mix. Toss the potatoes until coated in the seasoned oil.

5 Add a drizzle of olive oil and the butter to a skillet with a lid and place on medium heat. Add the potatoes and fry for 8 minutes, turning regularly. Cover with the lid and let the potatoes sweat for 5 minutes, then remove the lid, turn the heat up to high and cook for a final 5 minutes, until golden all over.

6 Serve the wraps with a little more sour cream, if liked, some fresh tomatoes, and chopped chives sprinkled on top. Finish with the potatoes and wedges of lime on the side.

Vegetarian Full English Breakfast Terrine

The idea of a terrine is quite retro, but remember I'm a child of the '70s and '80s! It has all the elements of a classic full English breakfast, just delivered in slice form, and if you've never tried cream cheese mixed with baked beans, then quite frankly, you haven't lived! If you prefer, swap the veggie sausages for a meaty alternative.

Serves 8–10

drizzle of olive oil, plus extra
    for greasing
2 vegetarian sausages (or
    meaty alternative)
6 hash browns
1lb 5oz (600g) mushrooms,
    roughly chopped
1 tsp finely chopped rosemary
    leaves
4 large eggs
splash of whole milk
8oz (226g) can baked beans
14oz (400g) cream cheese
1lb 2oz (500g) spinach leaves
salt and freshly ground
    black pepper
slices of toast, to serve

YOU WILL NEED
large baking sheet
small baking sheet, about the
    same size as the loaf pan,
    lightly oiled
10 x 4½ in (25 x 11 cm) loaf
    pan, oiled, and lined with
    plastic wrap, leaving an
    overhang

1 Preheat the oven to 400°F (200°C). Drizzle a little olive oil over a large baking sheet and place the sausages, hash browns, and mushrooms on the sheet. Scatter over the rosemary, then season with salt and pepper. Drizzle with a little more oil and cook in the oven for 25–35 minutes, until everything is beautifully golden. Set aside to cool.

2 Meanwhile, in a bowl, beat the eggs with a splash of milk. Season with salt and pepper, then pour the mixture into a small, oiled baking sheet. Place in the oven, below the baking sheet, and cook for 8 minutes, or until set. Set aside to cool.

3 In a large bowl, mix the baked beans with the cream cheese. Set aside.

4 Place a skillet on medium heat and add a drizzle of olive oil. Add the spinach, cover with a lid, and cook for 8 minutes, or until the leaves have wilted. Season with salt and pepper, and let the spinach cool.

5 Once everything is cooked and cooled, you're ready to build the terrine. Cut the sausages in half lengthwise and lay them, cut-side up, in the bottom of the lined loaf pan. Next, add half of the bean and cream cheese mixture, spreading it out evenly. Spoon half of the spinach evenly on top.

6 Cut the baked omelet in half lengthwise and lay one half on top of the spinach, followed by the remaining beany cream cheese, and a layer of hash browns. Spoon the remaining spinach over, followed by all the mushrooms. Top with a final layer of the baked omelet. Fold the overhanging plastic wrap tightly over the top of the terrine and place two heavy weights on top. Place the terrine in the fridge and let set for at least 8 hours, preferably overnight.

7 To serve, peel back the top layer of plastic wrap, lay a cutting board on top and flip it over. Carefully lift off the loaf pan and gently peel back the plastic wrap. Cut into thick slices and serve on toast.

Baked "Shakshuka" Tarts

Baking eggs in this Middle Eastern-inspired spicy tomato sauce takes them to another level, while the crispy crunch of the phyllo pastry shells brings so much acoustic joy. Cooking the tarts in a muffin pan is a great way to serve multiple people the same dish with no fuss. You can also adapt the quantity you make, depending on the size of the gathering and your muffin pan. The spicy tomato sauce can be made ahead and kept in the fridge or freezer (see below).

Makes 9

9oz (250g) package of phyllo
　pastry (you need 9 sheets)
olive oil, for brushing
9 eggs
3½oz (100g) feta cheese,
　crumbled
chopped cilantro, to serve

For the spicy tomato sauce:
(makes about 1¼ cups/300ml)

drizzle of extra-virgin olive oil
½ onion, finely chopped
2 garlic cloves, finely grated
1 red bell pepper, seeded and
　finely chopped
1 tsp ground cumin
1 tsp paprika
1 tsp chile flakes
2 x 14.5oz (411g) cans
　chopped tomatoes
1¼ cups (300ml) vegetable
　stock
1 tsp tomato paste
1 tbsp red wine vinegar
pinch of sugar
salt and freshly ground
　black pepper

YOU WILL NEED
9-hole muffin pan, brushed
　liberally with olive oil

1. Start with the spicy tomato sauce (it can be made up to 3 days in advance and kept in the fridge or frozen for 3 months; defrost thoroughly before use). Heat a little extra-virgin olive oil in a casserole dish on medium heat. Add the onion and sauté, stirring often, for 6 minutes, until softened. Stir in the garlic, red bell pepper, and the spices, and cook gently for a further 4 minutes, or until the onion starts to color and the pepper is soft.

2. Pour in the canned tomatoes, then refill the cans with the stock, swish around to remove any tomatoey residue and add to the dish. Stir in the tomato paste, vinegar, and sugar, then season well with salt and pepper. Let the sauce come up to a boil, then turn the heat down to the lowest setting, and gently simmer for 1 hour, until thickened and reduced by half. Let the sauce cool.

3. Preheat the oven to 350°F (180°C). To make the phyllo shells, unroll the pastry sheets and cut one into quarters. Brush each quarter of phyllo liberally with olive oil and carefully press them into one of the muffin cups in the pan, overlapping the pastry slightly as you work around the cup until the base and sides are lined. Repeat to make 9 phyllo shells in total.

4. Once all the muffin cups are lined with phyllo, carefully spoon in the cooled, spicy tomato sauce, until roughly filled by half. Crack an egg into each muffin cup on top of the sauce.

5. Place the muffin pan in the oven and bake for 20–25 minutes, or until the eggs are cooked to your liking, and the phyllo is golden and crisp. Remove from the oven and crumble over the feta cheese. Season with salt and pepper and finish with a sprinkling of cilantro.

Upside Down French Toast

I absolutely love French toast, but frustratingly, The Viking isn't a fan of sweet things for breakfast or brunch, so we rarely have it. This upside-down version is a wonderfully sweet and jammy mess of a dish, and the great thing is that you can make it as big or as small as you like—a whole tray for a large gathering or a single slice as a mini feast just for you.

Serves 4

4 large eggs
⅓ cup (100ml) whole milk
1 tsp vanilla extract
½ tsp ground cinnamon
maple syrup, for drizzling
5 tbsp (75g) salted butter
1 cup (100g) chopped walnuts
⅔ cup (100g) strawberries,
   hulled and cut in half
⅔ cup (100g) blueberries
4 thick slices of brioche
⅓ cup (75g) demerara sugar
powdered sugar, for dusting
   (optional)
whipped cream to serve

YOU WILL NEED
large baking sheet, roughly
   15 x 10½ in (38 x 27 cm),
   lined with parchment paper

1   Preheat the oven to 400°F (200°C). Crack the eggs into a large bowl and whisk in the milk, vanilla, and cinnamon. Set aside.

2   Drizzle the lined baking sheet with a generous amount of maple syrup, then dot small pieces of the butter all over. Scatter over the walnuts and half of the strawberries and blueberries (dot them randomly over the tray).

3   Dip the slices of brioche into the egg mixture and place them on top of the berries and nuts. (I prefer to slightly overlap the slices in a random pattern to allow the corners and edges sticking up to become extra golden and crunchy.) Sprinkle the top with demerara sugar.

4   Bake for 20–25 minutes, until the top of the bread is golden. Remove the brioche from the oven and let it sit on the tray for 5 minutes. Lay a piece of parchment paper on top, followed by a cutting board and carefully flip it over. Remove the tray and peel off the backing paper.

5   Decorate the top of the brioche with the remaining berries, a good drizzle of maple syrup, and a dusting of powdered sugar, if liked. Serve with whipped cream by the side.

Mimosa Swirl Buns

I like to accompany a special brunch with a mimosa (or a buck's fizz as it's known here in the UK). This classic, tipsy orange juice cocktail is the perfect way to start celebrating early! These swirly buns capture all the flavor and sparkle of a classic mimosa but in glorious dough form.

Makes 6

For the buns:
scant 1 cup (200ml) whole milk
5 tbsp (75g) unsalted butter, plus extra for greasing
finely grated zest of 1 orange
⅓ cup (100ml) sparkling wine
4 cups (500g) strong white bread flour, plus extra for dusting
2½ tbsp (30g) sugar
1 tsp salt
1 package (7g) instant dried yeast (2¼ tsp)
1 large egg, lightly beaten

For the filling:
½ cup (100g) light brown sugar
finely grated zest of 3 oranges
6 tbsp (100g) unsalted butter, softened and cut into cubes

For the glaze:
5½oz (150g) cream cheese
2–3 tbsp powdered sugar, sifted
splash of sparkling wine
finely grated zest of 1 orange

YOU WILL NEED
12 x 8 in (30 x 20 cm) baking dish, greased, and base-lined with parchment paper

1   First, start the bun dough. Heat the milk, butter, and orange zest in a small saucepan over medium-low heat until the butter melts. Let cool until just lukewarm, then pour in the sparkling wine—it may curdle a bit, but that is fine.

2   Mix the flour, sugar, salt, and yeast in a large bowl. Make a well in the middle, then pour in the lukewarm milk mixture and add the egg. Mix with your hands to form a rough, soft dough. Tip the dough out onto a lightly floured work surface and knead for 10–15 minutes, until smooth and elastic. (You can also do this in a stand mixer, using the dough hook on low speed for 10 minutes.) Place the dough in a lightly greased, clean bowl, cover with plastic wrap and let rise in a warm place for 2 hours, or until doubled in size.

3   Meanwhile, make the filling. Place the brown sugar and orange zest in a bowl, then rub together using your fingertips to release the essential oils in the zest. Add the butter and mix well until combined to a paste. Set aside.

4   Once the dough has risen, tip it out onto a lightly floured work surface and use a rolling pin to roll it into a 15 x 19 in (40 x 50 cm) rectangle. Using a spoon or spatula, spread the orange butter in an even layer over the surface of the dough. Working from one of the long sides, roll up the dough into a cylinder, keeping the spiral tight. Using a sharp knife, cut the dough into 6 thick, even slices.

5   Arrange the buns, cut-side up, snugly in the base of the greased and lined baking dish. Cover the dish with plastic wrap and let the buns prove for 45–60 minutes, until risen and puffy.

6   Preheat the oven to 350°F (180°C). Once proved, bake the buns for 30–40 minutes, or until risen and golden brown. While the buns are baking, prepare the glaze. Mix all the ingredients in a bowl until you have a thin icing.

7   Remove the buns from the oven and let them sit for 10 minutes in the dish on a wire rack. Drizzle or spread the icing over the top of each warm bun in a swirly pattern before serving.

Picni

Lun

cs &
ches

Growing up in 70s suburban London, our family picnics were not made up of cucumber sandwiches served from a wicker basket while sitting on a blanket on a grassy hillock. We did, however, have the occasional huddle behind a windbreak on Scarborough Beach with some sandwiches served out of a Tupperware box. Mum preferred to cater for a summer party at home, with guests choosing from a table (indoors) laden with her version of picnic delights: classic finger foods, robust pastry-filled items, sandwiches, and quiches galore. While my family didn't necessarily embrace the outdoorsy picnic life, we knew how to eat a good spread of picky bits, and that's what I'm celebrating in this chapter.

Three Dips in 90 Seconds

What's a picnic without a dip? These three dips are ridiculously simple to make, and hands down taste better than anything store-bought. I'm serving them with my Poppy & Fennel Seed Crackers (see p51) and Cheat's Ciabatta Crostini (see p52), which are drenched in herby oil, before being toasted in the oven until crisp and golden.

Serves about 10

YOU WILL NEED
blender or food processor, baking sheet

Cheese & Onion Dip

I use cottage cheese for this, which has a slight sharpness that works with the green onion, chives, and Cheddar cheese. Don't worry if you're not a fan of the texture of cottage cheese, blending turns it thick, creamy, and smooth.

Ingredients
10oz (300g) cottage cheese
1 bunch of fresh chives
½ green onion
2½oz (75g) sharp Cheddar
 cheese, cut into small pieces
1 tbsp olive oil, plus extra
 to serve
salt and freshly ground
 black pepper

Place everything in a blender or food processor and whizz until smooth and creamy. Season with salt and pepper, to taste. Spoon into a bowl, drizzle with extra olive oil and top with a grinding of black pepper, to serve.

My Tzatziki

You don't even need a blender to make this. Simply stir the ingredients together and tah dah—you have a creamy, herby, zesty dip.

Ingredients
10oz (300g) Greek yogurt
¼ cucumber, cut into very
 small dice
1 tbsp chopped dill
½ tbsp chopped mint leaves
finely grated zest of ½ lime
½ tsp garlic salt
1 tbsp olive oil

Place everything in a bowl (setting aside some of the cucumber and dill to serve) and mix well until combined. Spoon into a serving bowl and top with the reserved cucumber and dill.

Olive & Chickpea Tapenade

Tapenade with a twist, thanks to the addition of garlic-stuffed green olives and chickpeas—all blended into a dip.

Ingredients
8 garlic-stuffed green olives
⅔ cup (100g) canned
 chickpeas, drained
large handful of cilantro
2 tbsp olive oil, plus extra
 for drizzling
salt and freshly ground
 black pepper

Place everything in a food processor and pulse until roughly combined to a thick paste. Season with salt and pepper, to taste. Spoon into a serving bowl and drizzle with a little extra olive oil.

Poppy & Fennel Seed Crackers

I'd never thought of making crackers before, which is utterly insane as we get through a huge amount of cheese in this household, and a cracker is the ultimate vehicle to get said cheese into one's chops. These little beauties are easy to make, and you can be quite inventive with the flavorings—just remember to keep it simple and elegant.

Makes about 20

2 cups (250g) all-purpose flour, plus extra for rolling
¼ cup (50g) whole-wheat or rye flour
2 tsp baking powder
6 tbsp (85g) salted butter, softened and cut into small pieces
2 tsp fennel seeds
2 tsp poppy seeds
½ tsp flaky sea salt

YOU WILL NEED

large baking sheet, lined with parchment paper
fluted cutting wheel or cookie cutters of your choice

1 Preheat the oven to 350°F (180°C).

2 Place both types of flour, the baking powder, butter, fennel and poppy seeds, and salt in a food processor and blitz to a crumbly mixture. Add ⅓ cup (100ml) water and pulse again until the mixture comes together into a dough.

3 Roll the dough out on a lightly floured work surface until about ¼ in (5 mm) thick. Cut the dough into your choice of shapes and sizes; I use a fluted cutting wheel to do this, adding to their homemade appeal, but you could use a round fluted cookie cutter, if preferred. Space the crackers out on the lined baking sheet and prick the tops all over with a fork.

4 Bake for 15–20 minutes, until the crackers start to crisp and turn golden around the edges; they may still be slightly soft but will firm up further when cold. Let cool on the baking sheet.

5 Serve with dips (see p48), chopped liver (p109), or the cheese of your choice. The crackers will keep in an airtight container for up to 1 week.

Cook's Tip:

Try experimenting with different flavor combinations, including:
Rosemary and garlic salt
Thyme and lemon zest
Oregano & chile (both dried)

Cheat's Ciabatta Crostini

Need something to dunk into my dips (see p48) but don't have time to make crostini from scratch? This cheat's version still gives a homemade feel but in next to no time. I've made these with gluten-free ciabatta and regular ciabatta, and both work well.

Makes about 20

⅓ cup (100ml) extra virgin
   olive oil or cold-pressed
   canola oil
1 tbsp finely chopped rosemary
   leaves
1 tbsp finely chopped thyme
   leaves
½ tsp garlic salt
2 ciabatta loaves, thinly sliced
salt and freshly ground
   black pepper

YOU WILL NEED
1–2 large baking sheets

1　Preheat the oven to 375°F (190°C).

2　Mix the olive oil with the herbs and garlic salt in a large bowl. Season with salt and pepper, then add the slices of ciabatta. Mix well to coat the ciabatta in the herby, garlicky oil.

3　Arrange the ciabatta slices over the baking sheet(s) and bake for 10–15 minutes, turning halfway, until toasted and golden. Let cool on the baking sheet. Transfer the crostini to an airtight container and store for up to 2 days.

Grandma Sylvia's Cucumber Salad

My grandma, Sylvia, was a remarkable woman. A doctor's wife, she was fiercely intelligent and independent for a woman born at the turn of the last century. Her meals were hearty, homey, and delicious, and her cucumber salad was legendary! This is a traditional Jewish salad often served with salmon. It has Polish and Russian roots and would have originally used acetic acid, which you had to buy from the chemist. It's quite hard to find these days, so I've adapted it to the more widely available white wine vinegar.

Serves 6–8

1 whole cucumber
⅓ cup (60g) sugar
½ cup (120ml) warm water
2 tsp white wine vinegar
pinch of salt

YOU WILL NEED
mandolin or food processor

1   Slice the cucumber very finely into rounds or strips—a mandolin will make light work of this, but a food processor is safer! Place the cucumber in a large serving bowl.

2   In a small bowl, add the sugar and warm water, stir until dissolved, then let the water cool. Stir in the vinegar and salt, then pour the mixture over the sliced cucumber. Let the salad sit for at least 30 minutes before serving. It will stay fresh in the fridge for up to 4 days stored in an airtight container.

My Potato Salad

There's a trend for fancy potato salads, from roasted and smashed to fully mashed, but what I haven't seen is a classic, creamy mayonnaise potato salad—the kind Mum used to make when we were kids. Here, the potatoes are boiled until soft, but not falling apart, and the mayonnaise is more like a dressing than a condiment, loosened with a splash of vinegar and water so it's not too thick. Delicious.

Serves 6

1lb 10oz (750g) baby new
    potatoes, cut in half
5 green onions, thinly sliced
handful of mint leaves, finely
    chopped (optional)

**For the mayonnaise
dressing:**
2 egg yolks
1 heaped tsp Dijon mustard
½ tsp salt
1 tsp sugar
⅔ cup (140ml) cold-pressed
    canola oil
3 tsp white wine vinegar
2 tsp lemon juice

YOU WILL NEED
immersion blender

1   Cook the potatoes in a large saucepan of salted boiling water until tender but not too soft. Drain the potatoes thoroughly and transfer them to a large serving bowl.

2   Meanwhile, make the mayonnaise dressing. Using an immersion blender, blend all the ingredients with 1 tablespoon of water until smooth. It should emulsify into a creamy, yet loose, dressing.

3   Pour the dressing into the bowl of potatoes, add the green onions, and mix well until combined. Garnish with mint, if using, and serve while still warm, if possible.

Upside Down Caprese Salad in a Jar

I adore this all-in-one salad in a jar; it makes picnics so easy, and there's also a little hint of drama as you turn the jar upside down to release the contents into a serving bowl. Good-quality, vine-ripened tomatoes are essential, and a classic vinaigrette is a must.

Serves 2

4 tbsp extra virgin olive oil
1 tsp Dijon mustard
1 tsp dried oregano
2 tbsp apple cider vinegar
2 large heirloom tomatoes,
 thickly sliced
3½oz (100g) cherry tomatoes,
 quartered (I like to use
 orange or yellow ones)
1 large bunch of basil leaves
2 large balls of mozzarella,
 4oz (125g) each, drained
 and thickly sliced
1 large red onion, thinly sliced
 into rings
salt and freshly ground
 black pepper

YOU WILL NEED
4 cup (1 liter) large jar
 with lid

1 Add the olive oil, mustard, oregano, and vinegar to a jug, then mix together with a fork to make a dressing. Season with salt and pepper.

2 Arrange a layer of tomato (both sliced and quartered) in a 4 cup (1 liter) jar, followed by some basil leaves, and a layer of mozzarella. Add a layer of onion rings, then drizzle over some of the dressing. Repeat this layering until the jar is full, occasionally adding more of the dressing.

3 Put the lid on the jar and store the salad in the fridge. It will keep for up to 8–12 hours, but it is is good to eat immediately. When ready to serve, open the jar and flip it over to tip the salad into a bowl.

Roasted Beets, Feta & Green Bean Salad

Don't get me wrong, a sandwich has its place as part of a picnic, but I think a glorious salad can also be given room to shine. Both the beets and green beans in this salad can be prepared in advance and then put into a container for transporting. Assemble the salad once you're ready to eat.

Serves 6

For the roasted beets:
5 small raw beets, cut
   into wedges
½ red onion, cut into wedges
2 tbsp balsamic vinegar
2 tbsp cold-pressed
   canola oil
1 tsp Dijon mustard
salt and freshly ground
   black pepper

For the green beans:
7oz (200g) fine green beans
1 tbsp cold-pressed
   canola oil
finely grated zest and juice
   of 1 unwaxed lemon

To serve
4 cup (80g) bag of arugula,
   watercress, or spinach salad
5½oz (150g) feta cheese,
   crumbled
sesame seeds, for sprinkling

YOU WILL NEED
roasting pan

1   Preheat the oven to 375°F (190°C).

2   First prepare the roasted beets. Place the beets in a roasting pan with the rest of the ingredients and mix well. Season with salt and pepper. Roast the beets for roughly 45 minutes, turning regularly, until they are tender. Set aside to cool for 20 minutes.

3   Meanwhile, boil or steam the green beans until tender, roughly 4 minutes. Drain the beans well, if needed, and tip them into a bowl. While still warm, add the oil, and the zest and juice of the lemon. Stir well and set aside to cool.

4   To build your salad, add a base layer of salad leaves to a dish, top with the dressed green beans and then the roasted beets. Finish the salad with the crumbled feta cheese and a sprinkling of sesame seeds. Season with salt and pepper before serving.

The Best Ever Sausage Rolls

Sausage rolls always make an appearance when I'm making food for a picnic—and these ones are special, or so I'm told by friends who've tried them. They can be made meaty or vegetarian; simply swap out the pork sausages for your favorite vegetarian alternative. I recommend you go all out and make the "Ruff" Puff Pastry (see p12), although an all-butter, store-bought alternative would also work well.

Makes about 24

1 recipe quantity of "Ruff" Puff Pastry (see p12) or 2 premade 9¾ x 10½ in sheets of puff pastry rolled to 14 x 9 in (35 x 23 cm)
3oz (85g) package of sage and onion stuffing mix
drizzle of olive oil
5 tbsp (75g) salted butter
1 large onion, finely chopped
7oz (200g) brown mushrooms, finely chopped
1 tbsp chopped herbs, such as rosemary and thyme
2 large garlic cloves, crushed
6 pork (or vegetarian) sausages
3½oz (100g) sharp Cheddar cheese, grated
1 tsp English mustard
1 egg, lightly beaten
salt and freshly ground black pepper

YOU WILL NEED
large baking sheet, roughly 15 x 10½ in (38 x 27 cm), lined with parchment paper

1 Preheat the oven to 350°F (180°C). Make the pastry following the instructions on page 12 or use premade. Place in the fridge until needed.

2 Make the stuffing mix in a large bowl according to the package instructions, adding a drizzle of olive oil. Set aside.

3 Heat a drizzle of olive oil and the butter in a large skillet on medium heat. Add the onion and cook, stirring occasionally, for 5 minutes, then add the mushrooms and cook for a further 4 minutes. Stir in the herbs and garlic. Season with salt and pepper and cook for a final 5 minutes, until everything has softened and any liquid from the mushrooms has evaporated. Set aside.

4 Squeeze the sausages out of their skins into a large bowl and mash the sausage meat with the back of a fork. Add the stuffing, the mushroom mixture, and Cheddar cheese, and mix well. Set aside to cool.

5 Roll out 2 long strips of pastry, roughly 12 x 3¼ in (30 x 8 cm). (Save any leftover pastry for another recipe.) Spread the mustard over one side of each strip.

6 Split the sausage mixture in half and shape each half into a long log shape down the middle of each pastry strip. Wet the edges of the pastry with a little water before rolling them up, ensuring that the sealed edge is running along the bottom. Cut each roll into bite-sized slices, each about 1¼ in (3 cm). Brush the tops with egg and score each roll three times.

7 Place the sausage rolls on the lined baking sheet and bake for 30 minutes, until golden and risen. Turn off the heat and leave the sausage rolls in the oven for 10 minutes to cool slightly before serving.

Upside Down Scotch Egg Tart

The brilliant thing about a Scotch egg, much like a Cornish pasty, is that it's almost a meal in itself. For those not in the know, it's a hard-boiled egg, wrapped in sausage meat, coated in breadcrumbs, and then deep-fried until golden and crisp. It's a classic British picnic item, and this is my upside-down tart version. It's delicious served with chutney or my Red Onion Jam (see p15).

Serves 6

6 large eggs, at room
 temperature
2 premade 9¾ x 10½ in
 sheets of puff pastry or use
 homemade (see p12) rolled
 to 14 x 9 in (35 x 23 cm)
6 tbsp olive oil
1 tsp chopped rosemary
1 cup (125g) fresh breadcrumbs
14oz (400g) sausage meat,
 from inside of 6 sausages
1 egg, lightly beaten
salt and freshly ground
 black pepper

YOU WILL NEED
large baking sheet, roughly
 15 x 10½ in (38 x 27 cm),
 lined with parchment paper
3 in (7.5 cm) round cutter

1 Bring a small saucepan of water to a boil on high heat. Using a spoon, gently lower the eggs into the pan, reduce the heat by half and gently boil for 5 minutes. Immediately remove the eggs from the pan into a bowl of ice water. Allow them to cool for at least 10 minutes, then peel and set aside.

2 Preheat the oven to 350°F (180°C). Unroll the pastry and set aside.

3 Mark out a large rectangle on the parchment paper, the same size as the pastry. Using the cutter as a template, draw 6 disks evenly spaced apart on the paper. Place the paper drawn-side down on the baking sheet. Drizzle each of the 6 disks marked on the paper with half of the olive oil and sprinkle with rosemary. Season with salt and pepper.

4 Spoon the breadcrumbs over the marked circles in a pile (roughly 3 tbsp per circle). Drizzle the remaining oil over the breadcrumbs, then top with a hard-boiled egg.

5 Divide the sausage meat into 6 portions. Wrap a portion of sausage meat around each of the hard-boiled eggs until enclosed in an even layer. Place an egg on top of each breadcrumb pile.

6 Drape the pastry sheet over the top to cover and press the pastry down between each sausage meat-covered egg. Using the back of a spoon, scallop the edge of the pastry sheet to seal. Score the top in a diamond pattern with a sharp knife and then brush with egg.

7 Bake for 30 minutes, until the pastry is golden and crisp. Remove the tart from the oven and let it sit on the tray for 10 minutes. Lay a piece of parchment paper on top, followed by a cutting board, and carefully flip the tart over in one swift move. Remove the tray and peel off the backing paper. Cut into 6 squares to serve.

Upside Down Smoked Salmon & Spinach Mini Quiches

No picnic or summer spread is complete without quiche. Mum has always been exceptional at preparing quiches, and they always make an appearance at gatherings. She makes multiple versions, then has them ready to go in the freezer. My upside-down version is so simple to make, and can also be frozen, ready for picnics to come.

Makes 6

2 premade 9¾ x 10½ in
    sheets of puff pastry or use
    homemade (see p12) rolled
    to 14 x 9 in (35 x 23 cm)
2 eggs, lightly beaten, plus
    1 extra for glazing
1 tbsp cream cheese
2 tbsp Greek yogurt
1 large handful of fresh dill,
    chopped
3½oz (100g) smoked salmon,
    chopped
2½ cups (75g) spinach leaves,
    finely chopped
drizzle of olive oil
1 tsp fresh thyme leaves
finely grated zest of 1 unwaxed
    lemon
salt and freshly ground
    black pepper

YOU WILL NEED
large baking sheet, roughly
    15 x 10½ in (38 x 27 cm),
    lined with parchment paper
4 in (10 cm) cookie cutter

1   Preheat the oven to 425°F (220°C). Unroll the pastry and, using the cookie cutter, stamp out 6 rounds. Place them on a tray in the fridge until needed.

2   Using the same cookie cutter as a template, draw 6 rounds onto the sheet of parchment paper, evenly spaced apart. Place the paper drawn-side down on the baking sheet.

3   In a large bowl, beat 2 eggs, then add the cream cheese and yogurt. Season with salt and pepper, and stir in the dill to combine. Mix in the smoked salmon and spinach. Set aside.

4   Drizzle olive oil over the circles on the lined baking sheet and sprinkle with thyme and lemon zest. Season with salt and pepper. Divide the quiche filling between the marked rounds, leaving a narrow border—don't worry if any liquid seeps out.

5   Drape the pastry disks over the quiche filling. Using the back of a teaspoon, scallop the edges of the pastry to seal. Score a cross in the top of each quiche with a sharp knife and then brush with egg.

6   Bake for 25–35 minutes, until the pastry is golden and crisp. Remove the quiches from the oven and let them sit on the baking sheet for 5 minutes. Slide a spatula underneath each one and deftly flip them over to serve.

Plowman's Lunch Picnic Loaf

I'm definitely a picnic person over a barbecue one; I've always found barbecues to be a bit of an effort. I'd rather cook everything indoors and then transport it to a freshly mown lawn or to the beach to eat. And that's where this fabulous picnic loaf comes in. I've gone for the classic British flavors of a plowman's, layered inside a large loaf. The joy of this is that it can—and should—be made the day before, to allow the flavors time to meld together. Pure picnic joy!

Makes 1 large, filled loaf

1 large, round, crusty loaf (or
   My No-Knead "Sourdough"
   Bread on pages 16–17)
1 tbsp English mustard
2 tbsp mayonnaise
1 small Little Gem lettuce,
   leaves separated
6 slices of ham (I love a
   thick cut)
2 tbsp horseradish sauce
½ small cucumber, thinly sliced
5½oz (150g) sharp Cheddar
   cheese, thinly sliced
2 tbsp tangy chutney or
   British-style pickle spread
1 Scotch egg
3½oz (100g) premade coleslaw
4 mini pork pies
handful of pickles, such
   as baby pickled onions
   and cornichons
sea salt and freshly ground
   black pepper

1   Cut the top off your loaf to make a lid and scoop out most of the inside to leave room for the filling. (You can make breadcrumbs with the spare bread. It also freezes well.) Spread the inside of the loaf with half of the mustard and then half of the mayo.

2   Now, it's time to add the filling in layers. As with any good sandwich, it's important to consider structural integrity, so avoid layering slippery, moist things together. Remember to press down each layer as you go so that it's nice and firm, and to season with salt and pepper every few layers.

3   Add the layers in the following order (or you choose): lettuce leaves, ham, horseradish sauce, slices of cucumber, a third of the cheese, tangy chutney, a whole Scotch egg, another third of the cheese, coleslaw, whole pork pies, a handful of pickles to fill in the gaps, and the remaining cheese. Spread the rest of the mustard and mayonnaise over the bread "lid" and place it on top of the loaf. Wrap the whole thing tightly in plastic wrap and pop it in the fridge until ready to serve.

4   When ready to serve, cut the picnic loaf into slices or wedges. And devour!

Quiche Susanna

This quiche is named after our wonderful food stylist, Susanna, who has beautifully cooked the food and styled the photographs for this and my previous book. Along with the crispy lardons of the classic quiche Lorraine, this version is made with beet pastry and also features one of Sus' favorite vegetables, fennel. Sweet with a hint of aniseed, fennel is the perfect accompaniment to the salty bacon, making it my new favorite flavor combination.

Serves 8

For the beet pastry:
½ cup plus 2 tbsp (150g) cold salted butter, cut into cubes, plus extra for greasing
2¼oz (70g) cooked beets (not in vinegar), grated
½ cup plus 2 tbsp (150g) all-purpose flour
1 cup (100g) rye flour
1 tsp each of finely chopped thyme and rosemary leaves
pinch of salt

For the filling:
drizzle of olive oil
5½oz (150g) bacon, cut into cubes or lardons
1 fennel bulb, cut into thin wedges (don't trim)
1 tsp each of finely chopped thyme and rosemary leaves
4 eggs, lightly beaten
1 cup (225g) Greek yogurt
⅓ cup (100ml) whipping cream
salt and freshly ground black pepper
dill sprigs, to garnish

YOU WILL NEED
medium roasting pan
8in (20cm) fluted, loose-bottomed flan pan or tart dish, greased

1   Make the pastry. Place the butter, beets, both types of flour, the herbs, and a pinch of salt in a food processor and whizz to a crumbly consistency (it may clump slightly, which is fine). Add a splash of cold water and blitz again until the pastry comes together into a smooth ball of dough—you may need to add a little more water. Wrap the pastry in plastic wrap and chill for at least 30 minutes.

2   While the pastry is chilling, place a skillet on medium heat and add a drizzle of olive oil. Add the bacon and sauté, stirring regularly, for 8 minutes, or until golden and crisp. Lift out with a slotted spoon to drain on a plate, lined with paper towels, and set aside to cool.

3   Preheat the oven to 375°F (190°C). Place the fennel wedges in a roasting pan and sprinkle with the herbs. Season with a little salt and pepper and drizzle with olive oil. Stir well to coat the fennel in the seasoned oil and roast in the oven for 30 minutes, until tender but not too soft. Set aside.

4   Turn the oven down to 350°F (180°C). Remove the pastry from the fridge and roll it out on a lightly floured work surface into a round large enough to line the base and sides of the flan pan or tart dish, and about ⅛in (3mm) thick. Trim the edge of the pastry, prick the base with a fork, and line with a piece of parchment paper. Fill the lined pastry case with pie weights and blind bake for 15 minutes, or until slightly golden around the edges. Lift out the paper and pie weights, then return the pastry case to the oven for another 10 minutes, or until cooked.

5   Beat the eggs, yogurt, and cream in a bowl. Season with salt and pepper, and stir in the cooled crispy bacon.

6   Arrange the fennel in the pastry case, then pour in the egg and cream mixture. Bake for 45 minutes, until golden and risen. Set aside on a wire rack to cool slightly. Remove the quiche from the flan pan or tart dish, sprinkle with dill, and serve it cut into slices.

Upside Down Summer Berry Sandwich

Every picnic or lunch needs something sweet, and this incredible dessert takes the classic strawberries and cream to a new level. Berries tend to turn mushy in the oven, but this is no bad thing here. When roasted, they turn into a perfect, sticky, jammy filling for a creamy, summery, puff pastry indulgence.

Serves 2

2 premade 9¾ x 10½ in sheets of puff pastry or use homemade (see p12) rolled to 14 x 9 in (35 x 23 cm)
2 tbsp lemon and lime marmalade
3 tbsp honey
1 tbsp balsamic glaze
5½oz (150g) raspberries
3½oz (100g) blueberries
finely grated zest of 1 orange
1 egg, lightly beaten

For the topping:
1¼ cup (300ml) whipping cream
2 tbsp Greek yogurt
1 tbsp cream cheese
1 tbsp powdered sugar, plus extra for dusting
3½oz (100g) strawberries, hulled and cut in half

YOU WILL NEED
large baking sheet, roughly 15 x 10½ in (38 x 27 cm), lined with parchment paper

1   Preheat the oven to 425°F (220°C). Unroll the pastry and cut out two 5½ in (14 cm) squares. Spread 1 tablespoon of the lemon and lime marmalade over each square, leaving a narrow border around the edge. Place in the fridge until needed.

2   Mark out 2 squares on the parchment paper, the same size as the pastry and with space between each one, and place drawn-side down on the baking sheet. Drizzle the honey and balsamic glaze over. Divide the raspberries and blueberries between the 2 squares, piling them up in the center. Sprinkle with the orange zest.

3   Lay a square of pastry, marmalade-side down, over each pile of berries. Using the back of a teaspoon, scallop the edge of the pastry squares to seal. Score the top in a diamond pattern with a sharp knife and then brush with egg.

4   Bake for 25 minutes, until the pastry is golden and crisp. Remove the tarts from the oven and let them sit on the baking sheet for 5 minutes. Lay a piece of parchment paper on top, followed by a cutting board, and carefully flip the tarts over in one swift move. Remove the baking sheet and peel off the backing paper. Let cool.

5   Meanwhile, finish the topping. Pour the whipping cream into a bowl and whisk to soft peaks with an electric hand whisk. Stir in the yogurt, cream cheese, and sugar, and whisk again until firm but still soft and whippy.

6   Spoon the whipped cream over the two tarts, dividing it equally. Arrange the strawberries, cut-side down, on one of the tarts. Then place the second tart on top of the strawberries, cream-side down. Dust the top with powdered sugar and cut diagonally in half to serve.

Every
Feas

yday
ting

Clearly, life isn't one endless round of parties, picnics, and brunches, but this doesn't mean that we can't add a little pizzazz to the everyday. Whether it's a family meal or movie night for one, the plan is to make each day feel a little special. Here's a collection of my favorite comfort meals, some given an upside-down twist and others pure classics. A few are slightly more time-consuming to make and perfect for weekends, while others take less time to prepare and are suitable for weekdays—all are easy, shareable, and generous. Perfect for everyday feasting.

Upside Down Carrot & Cilantro Tart

People sometimes ask, "Is there anything you can't turn upside down?" My answer is perhaps obvious—soup! Yet, I can still capture the flavors of my favorite soups in a tart. Carrot and cilantro is a classic combination that works wonderfully cooked this way.

Serves 4

2 premade 9¾ x 10½ in sheets of puff pastry or use homemade (see p12) rolled to 14 x 9in (35 x 23 cm)
drizzle of olive oil
drizzle of honey
1 tsp thyme leaves, plus extra to serve
6 carrots, halved lengthwise
1 egg, lightly beaten
salt and freshly ground black pepper

For the cilantro pesto:
1 large handful of cilantro leaves and stalks
½ cup (50g) walnuts
1 garlic clove
2¾oz (80g) sharp Cheddar cheese, coarsely grated
2 tbsp olive oil

YOU WILL NEED
large baking sheet, roughly 15 x 10½in (38 x 27 cm), lined with parchment paper

1   Preheat the oven to 425°F (220°C). Unroll the pastry and set aside.

2   Mark out a 14 x 9in (35 x 23 cm) rectangle on the parchment paper, and place it drawn-side down on the baking sheet. Drizzle olive oil and honey over the lined baking sheet, then sprinkle with the thyme. Season with salt and pepper.

3   Leaving a ¾in (2 cm) border, arrange the carrots cut-side down in 2 tight rows on the marked rectangle—each row of carrots should be placed lengthwise on the parchment paper with the pointed ends facing toward the middle.

4   Place all the ingredients for the cilantro pesto in a food processor and blitz to a coarse paste. Leaving a ½in (1 cm) border, spread the pesto over one side of the pastry.

5   Drape the pastry, pesto-side down, over the carrots. Using the back of a teaspoon, scallop the edges of the pastry to seal. Score the top in a diamond pattern with a sharp knife and then brush with egg.

6   Bake for 30 minutes, until the pastry is golden and crisp. Remove the tart from the oven and let it sit on the baking sheet for 5 minutes. Lay a piece of parchment paper on top, followed by a cutting board, and carefully flip it over. Remove the baking sheet and peel off the backing paper. Cut into quarters and serve sprinkled with extra thyme, if you like.

Upside Down Chicken Naan

Growing up, my local high street was home to many amazing Indian restaurants. The dishes I ate were often "tame" versions of traditional ones, as the originals were said to be too spicy or unusual for our unaccustomed palates. A lot has changed since, but I still adore a classic takeout curry, and this one is inspired by a recipe from my friend, chef and "fakeaway" expert, Dean Edwards.

Serves 4

2 tbsp (25g) ghee or vegetable oil
3 onions, sliced
2 carrots, diced
1 small red bell pepper, diced
2 tsp garlic paste
2 tsp ginger paste
2 tsp garam masala
¾ tsp ground turmeric
½ tsp paprika
¾ cup (200g) canned Roma
   tomatoes
2 tsp tomato paste

For the naan dough:
½ cup (120ml) warm water
1 package (7g) instant dried
   yeast (2¼ tsp)
2 tsp sugar
2⅓ cups (300g) strong white
   bread flour
½ tsp salt, plus extra to season
½ tsp baking powder
5 tbsp (75g) butter/ghee, melted
⅔ cup (150ml) plain yogurt
1 tbsp nigella seeds

For the topping:
1 onion, sliced
2 skinless, boneless chicken
   breasts, cut into chunks
freshly ground black pepper
1 handful of chopped cilantro

YOU WILL NEED
large baking sheet, roughly
   15 x 10½ in (38 x 27 cm),
   lined with parchment paper

1 To make the curry sauce, heat the ghee or vegetable oil in a large pan over a medium–low heat. Add the onions, carrots, red bell pepper, garlic, and ginger, and cook, stirring occasionally, for 20 minutes, until softened. Stir in the spices, canned tomatoes, and tomato paste, then pour in enough water to just cover the vegetables, about 1 cup (250ml). Cover with the lid and simmer for 30 minutes. Let cool, then blend until smooth.

2 Meanwhile, make the naan dough. Pour the warm water into a bowl and sprinkle over the yeast and half of the sugar. Leave for 10–15 minutes, until frothy. In a large bowl, mix together the flour, remaining sugar, the salt, and baking powder. Make a well in the center and pour in 2 tbsp (30g) of the melted butter or ghee, the yogurt, nigella seeds, and yeast mixture. Using your hands, bring the mixture together. Knead the dough in the bowl until it comes together into a ball, then tip it out onto a well-floured surface and knead for another 10 minutes, or until smooth and elastic. Put the dough in a greased bowl, cover, and let rise in a warm place for about 1 hour, until doubled in size.

3 Preheat the oven to 425°F (220°C). Leaving a ¾ in (2 cm) border, brush half of the remaining melted butter or ghee over the lined baking sheet and season with salt and pepper. Scatter over half of the sliced onion and one of the chicken breasts, then spoon half of the cooled curry sauce on top. Repeat with the rest of the onion, the second chicken breast, and the remaining sauce.

4 Tip the naan dough out onto a lightly floured surface and gently roll it out to a rectangle, about 16 x 11 in (40 x 28 cm). Carefully lay the naan over the top of the curry and tuck in the edges. Brush the top with the remaining melted butter or ghee.

5 Bake for 25 minutes, or until the naan is risen and golden. Remove the chicken curry naan from the oven and let it sit on the baking sheet for 10 minutes. Place a piece of parchment paper on top, followed by a cutting board and then carefully flip it over. Remove the baking sheet and peel off the backing paper. Sprinkle with chopped cilantro, to serve.

Upside Down Smashed Burger Tarts

There has been a big trend for smashed burgers in recent years and I can totally understand why—they're so simple and the "smashing" of the meat patty to flatten it out ensures a quick and even cook. My twist uses ready-made meatballs and, of course, puff pastry, which turns these into little pies. They are wonderful served warm from the oven, topped with pickles and your favorite sauces.

Makes 6

2 premade 9¾ x 10½ in
   sheets of puff pastry or use
   homemade (see p12) rolled
   to 14 x 9in (35 x 23 cm)
6 tbsp Red Onion Jam (see
   p15), or use store-bought
drizzle of olive oil
2 tsp thyme leaves
1 red onion, thinly sliced
   into rings
6 beef meatballs (I use
   ready-made ones—you could
   also use chicken or pork)
3½oz (100g) Cheddar cheese,
   finely grated
1 egg, lightly beaten
salt and freshly ground
   black pepper

To serve:
your choice of favorite pickles,
   mustard and ketchup, or
   any burger relish

YOU WILL NEED
large baking sheet, roughly
   15 x 10½ in (38 x 27 cm),
   lined with parchment paper
4 in (10 cm) cookie cutter

1 Preheat the oven to 425°F (220°C). Unroll the pastry and, using the cookie cutter, cut out 6 rounds. Slather each pastry round with 1 tablespoon of the onion jam, leaving a narrow border around the edge. Place them on a tray in the fridge until needed.

2 Using the same cookie cutter as a template, draw 6 circles onto the sheet of parchment paper, evenly spaced apart, and place drawn-side down on the baking sheet.

3 Drizzle oil over the drawn circles on the lined baking sheet and sprinkle with thyme. Season with salt and pepper, then scatter over the onion rings. Place a meatball in the middle of each circle and gently press it down to form a flat "burger" patty. Divide the grated cheese between the tarts, sprinkling it over the top of the smashed meatballs.

4 Drape the pastry disks, jam-side down, over the meatballs. Using the back of a fork, press around the edge of each pastry disk to seal. Score the tops in a diamond pattern with a sharp knife and then brush with egg.

5 Bake for 30–35 minutes, until the pastry is golden and crisp. Remove the tarts from the oven and let them sit on the baking sheet for 5 minutes. Slide a spatula underneath each one and deftly flip them over. Dress with your choice of pickles, mustard, ketchup, or any burger relish you love.

Upside Down Cheese & Pickle Sandwich

Picture the scene... it's late, you've made your way home after a night out with the gang, you're probably a little tipsy, and you haven't eaten. There's little food in the house, but you do have a bag of chips, a chunk of Cheddar cheese, and a jar of pickle that's been in the back of the fridge for a while, and, of course, if you're like me, a ubiquitous sheet of puff pastry. I present to you the puff pastry sandwich of joy!

Serves 2

2 premade 9¾ x 10½ in sheets of puff pastry or use homemade (see p12) rolled to 14 x 9in (35 x 23 cm)
2 tbsp tangy chutney
drizzle of olive oil
5½oz (150g) potato chips, any flavor, but I think salted is the best
3½oz (100g) sharp Cheddar, finely grated
1 egg, lightly beaten
salt and freshly ground black pepper

YOU WILL NEED
large baking sheet, roughly 15 x 10½in (38 x 27 cm), lined with parchment paper

1 Preheat the oven to 425°F (220°C). Unroll the pastry and cut out two 5½in (14 cm) squares. Spread 1 tablespoon of the tangy chutney over each square, leaving a narrow border. Place in the fridge until needed.

2 Mark out 2 squares on the parchment paper, the same size as the pastry and with space between each one, and place drawn-side down on the baking sheet. Drizzle with olive oil and season with salt and pepper.

3 Take half of the chips and scrunch them up into crumbs, then sprinkle over the drawn squares, leaving a ½in (1 cm) border around the edge. Add a generous pile of cheese over the crushed chips.

4 Lay a square of puff pastry, pickle-side down, over each pile of cheese. Using the back of a teaspoon, scallop the edges of the pastry to seal. Score the tops in a diamond pattern with a sharp knife and then brush with egg.

5 Bake for 25 minutes, until the pastry is golden and crisp. Remove the tarts from the oven and let them sit on the baking sheet for 5 minutes. Lay a piece of parchment paper on top, followed by a cutting board, and carefully flip the tarts over. Remove the baking sheet and peel off the backing paper.

6 Let the tarts cool for a further 5 minutes before scattering the remaining potato chips over one of the pastry squares. Slide a spatula underneath the other tart and flip it over on top of the first, then press down until you hear a crunch. Slice diagonally in half to serve.

Upside Down Mac 'n' Cheese Pie

The ultimate comfort food. Here, I'm dialing up the carbs with pasta *and* a layer of puff pastry. The trick to a good mac and cheese is to use two types of cheese. I go for something strong, like an extra-mature Cheddar, combined with a stringy, nutty cheese, such as Emmental, which works perfectly. Although, you could go with something even cheesier, like Velveeta, a classic brand of melting cheese, that is sinful, but really makes a difference.

Serves 4–6

2 premade 9¾ x 10½ in sheets of puff pastry or use homemade (see p12) rolled to 14 x 9in (35 x 23 cm)
7oz (200g) macaroni or fusilli
1 recipe quantity of Cheese Sauce (see p14)
7 bacon slices
drizzle of olive oil
1 cup (100g) breadcrumbs
1¾oz (50g) sharp Cheddar cheese, finely grated
1 egg, lightly beaten
salt and freshly ground black pepper
chopped chives, to garnish

YOU WILL NEED
large baking sheet, roughly 15 x 10½ in (38 x 27 cm), lined with parchment paper

1 Preheat the oven to 425°F (220°C). Unroll the pastry and set aside.

2 Cook the pasta in a saucepan of boiling salted water for half the time instructed on the package. Drain well and stir the pasta into the prepared cheese sauce.

3 Meanwhile, fry the bacon in a drizzle of olive oil in a skillet until dark and crispy. Remove the bacon from the pan, drain on paper towels, and chop it into small pieces. Mix the breadcrumbs with the cheese. Set aside.

4 Mark out a large rectangle on the parchment paper, the same size as the pastry, and place it drawn-side down on the baking sheet. Drizzle generously with olive oil, then season with salt and pepper.

5 Leaving a ½in (1 cm) border, sprinkle the cheesy breadcrumbs over the marked rectangle, then top with half of the crispy bacon. Spoon half of the mac and cheese over the bacon, making sure you keep it within the marked rectangle, then top with the rest of the bacon and the remaining mac and cheese.

6 Lay the pastry sheet over the mac and cheese. Using the back of a fork or teaspoon, press around the edges of the pastry to seal. Score the top in a diamond pattern with a sharp knife and then brush with beaten egg.

7 Bake for 25–30 minutes, until the pastry is golden and crisp. Remove the pie from the oven and let it sit on the baking sheet for 10 minutes. Lay a piece of parchment paper on top, followed by a cutting board, and carefully flip the tart over in one swift move. Remove the sheet and peel off the backing paper. Sprinkle with chives and cut into squares to serve.

Chicken & Chorizo Tarte Tatin

What I love most about chorizo is the wonderful garlicky, paprika-infused fat and color it releases when cooking. The popular Spanish sausage adds both a deep-red hue and a spicy smokiness to this savory version of the classic tart.

Serves 4

1 recipe quantity of Shortcrust Pie Dough (see p12) rolled to roughly 14 x 9 in (35 x 23 cm)
7oz (200g) dry-cured chorizo sausage, cut into thick slices
3 round shallots, peeled and cut in half lengthwise
1 tsp chopped thyme leaves, plus extra to serve
4 skinless, boneless chicken thighs, each cut into 4 large chunks
1 egg, lightly beaten
salt and freshly ground black pepper

YOU WILL NEED
8 in (20 cm) ovenproof skillet or cast-iron pan

1   Unroll the pastry as necessary and cut out a 9 in (23 cm) round; you may have to roll the pastry out slightly to ensure it is large enough. Place it in the fridge until needed.

2   Place the ovenproof skillet or pan on medium heat. Add the chorizo and sauté for roughly 5 minutes on each side until it starts to color and release its oil. Add the shallots, cut-side down, and scatter over half of the thyme. Cook for 5 minutes, turning halfway, until the shallots start to caramelize in the chorizo oil.

3   Next, add the chicken thighs to the pan and cook for a further 5 minutes, turning halfway, until colored on both sides. Arrange the ingredients in the pan so you have an even spread of chicken, chorizo, and shallots. Season with salt and pepper.

4   Meanwhile, preheat the oven to 400°F (200°C).

5   Remove the pastry round from the fridge and drape it over the ingredients in the pan, then carefully tuck in the edge of the pastry. Brush the top with egg and cut a slash with a sharp knife to make a hole for the steam to escape.

6   Bake for 25 minutes, or until the pastry is darkly golden and crisp. Let the tart sit for 5 minutes. Place a large platter on top of the pan and carefully flip the tart over, right-side up. Lift off the pan to reveal the tart, then sprinkle the top with the remaining thyme.

Deep-Pan Focaccia Pizza Pie

My husband, The Viking, is a fan of deep-pan pizza. I think it's his love of bread—after all, isn't this type of pizza essentially fluffy bread topped with tomato and cheese? This focaccia pizza pie is my compromise, and while it's a little time-consuming to make the dough, it's undeniably good. The deep, fluffy base can be topped with any of your favorite, fresh seasonal ingredients—I've gone for one that combines my Tomato & Olive Sauce (see p14) with Tuscan kale greens, and a mix of cheeses.

Serves 4

For the dough:
1 package (7g) instant dried
  yeast (2¼ tsp)
1½ tsp fine sea salt, plus extra
  to season
½ tsp sugar
1 tbsp olive oil
1¼ cups (300ml) lukewarm
  water
4 cups (500g) strong bread
  flour, plus extra for dusting
extra virgin olive oil, for
  greasing and drizzling

For the topping:
4–5 Tuscan kale leaves,
  depending on size, tough
  stalks removed, and leaves
  torn into small pieces
⅓ cup (100g) Tomato & Olive
  Sauce (see p14)
5½oz (150g) mozzarella,
  drained and torn into pieces
1¾oz (50g) sharp Cheddar
  cheese, grated
½ cup (100g) mixed olives,
  pitted
1 tbsp dried oregano
freshly ground black pepper

YOU WILL NEED
9 x 13in baking dish, greased
  generously

1 To make the dough, place all the ingredients, except the extra virgin olive oil, in a large bowl and bring them together into a rough ball with a spatula or your hand. Tip the dough out onto a lightly oiled surface and knead for 5 minutes, until it forms a shaggy, sticky ball. (This can also be done in a stand mixer with a dough hook.)

2 Generously oil the cleaned bowl (or use a large, lidded container). Place the dough in the bowl or container, cover with a damp dish towel or lid, and let rest for 30 minutes. Remove the dish towel/lid and, with damp hands, press your fingers into the dough, stretching and pulling it for about a minute. Cover the bowl/container and let the dough rest for another 30 minutes. Repeat this three more times, then let the dough rest for a final 1 hour, or until doubled in size.

3 Gently tip the risen dough into the baking dish and, using oiled fingers, press the dough out to cover the base, then press indentations over the top. Place a damp dish towel over the dish and let prove for 30 minutes.

4 Meanwhile, preheat the oven to 425°F (220°C).

5 To top the pizza pie, steam the kale leaves until wilted. Spread the tomato and olive sauce over the focaccia base, leaving a generous border. Scatter the mozzarella, half of the Cheddar cheese, and the kale over, then top with the olives and the remaining Cheddar. Using oiled fingers, gently press more indentations into the dough.

6 Sprinkle over the oregano and season with salt and plenty of pepper. Bake for 25 minutes, or until the crust is golden and puffy, and the cheese is wonderfully gooey. Lift the pizza out of the dish and serve cut into slices.

Cottage Pie with Carrot, Rutabaga & Potato Topping

I've upped the vegetables quota in this cottage pie by adding rutabaga and carrot to the mashed potato topping, which adds a different flavor dimension to the classic recipe. This is perfect warming, comfort food in one dish—all that's needed is to place the pie in the center of the table and let everyone help themselves.

Serves 4

For the filling:

3 tbsp (50g) salted butter
2 tbsp olive oil
1 onion, finely chopped
2 celery sticks, finely chopped
1 carrot, finely chopped
2 garlic cloves, grated
1 tsp chopped rosemary leaves
1 tsp chopped thyme leaves
10oz (300g) ground beef
1 tsp tomato paste
14.5oz (411g) can chopped
    tomatoes
2 cups (500ml) vegetable stock
4 tsp brown gravy mix
⅓ cup (100ml) white wine
½ cup (100g) frozen peas
salt and freshly ground pepper

For the topping:

2¼lb (1kg) potatoes, such as
    Russet, peeled and cut into
    large chunks
1 rutabaga, peeled and
    finely chopped
2 large carrots, finely chopped
3 tbsp (50g) salted butter
3½oz (100g) Cheddar cheese,
    grated

YOU WILL NEED
large, oval baking/pie dish

1 Preheat the oven to 400°F (200°C).

2 To make the filling, melt the butter and olive oil in a sauté pan on medium heat. Add the onion, celery, and carrot, and sauté for 5 minutes, until softened. Stir in the garlic and herbs and cook for an additional 5 minutes, stirring regularly to prevent the garlic from burning. Season with a little salt and pepper.

3 Add the ground beef and cook, stirring to break up any large clumps, for 6 minutes, or until it begins to brown. Stir in the tomato paste, canned tomatoes, stock, gravy mix, and wine. Bring to a gentle boil, then turn the heat down to low. Add the peas and gently simmer away for 15 minutes, until the sauce has reduced and thickened.

4 Meanwhile, make the mashed topping. I like to steam the vegetables because it creates a fluffier, less watery result. Add the chopped vegetables to a tiered steamer (I put the rutabaga in the bottom steamer basket, as it takes longer to cook, and the potatoes and carrots on top). Steam the vegetables for 10 minutes, until tender, then tip them into a large bowl, place a clean dish towel over the top, and let rest for 2 minutes—this will help to steam-dry the vegetables, ensuring a fluffy topping. Add the butter and mash well, then mix in the Cheddar cheese. Season with salt and pepper.

5 Tip the filling into the baking or pie dish and carefully spoon the mash mix on top. Run a fork over the topping to create a textured top (adding a few extra pieces of butter, if you like) and bake for 30 minutes, or until gloriously golden.

Cook's Tip:
You can prepare the topping up to 2 days in advance and keep it in the fridge. Alternatively, freeze for up to 3 months and defrost before use.

Prosecco Fish Pie

I absolutely love a fish pie, but I wanted to elevate it to a special occasion dish. It's not just the combination of salmon, shrimp, and smoked haddock, or the golden potato topping that makes this pie so exceptional, it's the creamy prosecco sauce that takes it to another fabulous level. There's something about the floral, fruity, citrus notes that just works, turning this humble favorite into a feast for friends.

Serves 4

For the potato topping:
1 tbsp olive oil
3 tbsp (40g) salted butter
5 large potatoes, diced
1 garlic clove, chopped
1 tsp thyme leaves

For the filling:
14oz (400g) skinless smoked
   haddock or cod
9oz (250g) skinless salmon
   fillets
2 cups (500ml) whole milk
⅓ cup (100ml) prosecco or
   other sparkling wine
3 tbsp (50g) salted butter
⅓ cup (50g) all-purpose flour
3½oz (100g) Cheddar cheese,
   finely grated
1 tsp Dijon mustard
½ cup (100g) frozen peas
6oz (175g) large, raw peeled
   shrimp, deveined
salt and freshly ground
   black pepper
chopped chives, to garnish
green salad, to serve

YOU WILL NEED
large ovenproof pie dish

1 To make the potato topping, place a large sauté pan (with a lid) on medium heat and add the olive oil and butter. Add the potatoes, garlic, and thyme. Cover the pan with the lid, turn the heat to low and steam-cook the potatoes for 8 minutes, until tender. Remove the lid, turn up the heat and sauté until the potatoes turn a gentle golden color. Remove the potatoes from the pan and set aside.

2 Put the haddock and salmon in the sauté pan and pour over the milk. Cover with the lid, turn the heat to medium and bring to a simmer. When the milk starts to bubble, turn the heat off and let the fish poach for 3 minutes. Gently remove the fish with a spatula (it should be slightly undercooked at this point), leaving the milk in the pan. Set aside the fish.

3 Place the pan containing the milk (there should be around 1¾ cups/400ml) back on medium heat. Pour in the prosecco or sparkling wine and mix in the butter and flour. Whisk gently for roughly 5 minutes until the butter melts and the sauce has thickened to a creamy consistency. Turn the heat to low and simmer gently for another 3 minutes, stirring occasionally. Stir in the Cheddar cheese and mustard, then season with salt and pepper. Remove the pan from the heat and stir in the peas and shrimp.

4 Preheat the oven to 375°F (190°C). Flake the poached salmon and haddock in large chunks into the large ovenproof dish. Pour the prosecco sauce over and gently mix until combined. Spoon the golden chunky potatoes on top. Bake for 15–20 minutes, until the potatoes turn crisp and a darker shade of golden. Serve with a sprinkling of fresh chopped chives and a green salad.

Steak, Ale & Shallot Pie

Pies remind me of cozy nights by the fire, being with family and loved ones, and act as a reminder to take things more slowly. They evoke feelings of nostalgia and comfort. This pie, with its caramelized shallot and potato topping, is a celebration of slower days, when the world can wait and we can all get together to enjoy a delicious meal.

Serves 4

2 tbsp all-purpose flour
2¼lb (1kg) beef shank, cut into
　large chunks
2 tbsp olive oil, plus extra for
　the potatoes
3 tbsp (40g) salted butter
14oz (400g) shallots, peeled
　and halved lengthwise
1 tbsp thyme leaves
1 tsp chopped rosemary leaves
2 garlic cloves, crushed
scant 1 cup (200ml) dark ale
1¾ cups (400ml) beef stock
1lb 2oz (500g) baby new
　potatoes, thickly sliced
　into rounds
salt and freshly ground
　black pepper
green beans, to serve

YOU WILL NEED
large, ovenproof pie dish

1　Start to make the filling. Place the flour in a large bowl and season with salt and pepper. Add the beef and turn to coat it in the seasoned flour.

2　Place a large sauté pan (with a lid) on medium heat. Add half of the olive oil and half of the butter to the pan with the beef and cook for roughly 5 minutes, turning occasionally, until browned all over. Remove from the pan with a slotted spoon onto a plate and set aside.

3　Add most of the remaining oil and butter to the pan with half of the shallots and cook for roughly 5 minutes, turning regularly. Add half of the thyme and cook for another 5 minutes, until the shallots are dark golden. Remove the shallots and set aside (these will be for the topping). Repeat with the remaining shallots and thyme, adding more oil and butter, if needed.

4　Return the browned beef to the pan containing half of the cooked golden shallots. Stir in the rosemary and garlic, and after a minute, add the ale and stock. Bring up to boiling point, then turn the heat down to low, cover with the lid, and let the stew gently bubble away for 1 hour.

5　Meanwhile, parboil the potatoes in a large saucepan of boiling salted water for 4 minutes, until softened but not fully cooked. Drain the potatoes well, then return them to the pan and douse in olive oil. Season with salt and pepper.

6　Preheat the oven to 375°F (190°C). Tip the pie filling into the large, ovenproof pie dish. Arrange the slices of potato and the reserved shallots on top (I like to do it with a ring of potatoes and then a ring of shallots, starting from the middle to the outer edge). Bake for 20 minutes, or until the top is golden and starting to crisp. Serve with green beans.

Upside Down Ratatouille Tart

I love experimenting with traditional dishes, especially if it allows me to use up what's left over in the fridge. With this dish, I'm drifting slightly from the classic and substituting red bell pepper with beets as that's what I had to hand. I genuinely believe that you use what you can, and that's how we evolve in the food world. You'll need my luscious Tomato & Olive Sauce for this (see p14).

Serves 6

2 premade 9¾ x 10½ in sheets of puff pastry or use homemade (see p12) rolled to 14 x 9in (35 x 23 cm)
3 tbsp olive oil
3 tbsp (50g) salted butter
1 tsp oregano leaves, plus extra to garnish
1 tsp thyme leaves
1 tsp rosemary leaves
2 tsp sweet smoked paprika
finely grated zest of ½ unwaxed lemon
1 long potato, cut into roughly ¼ in (5 mm) thick slices
2 medium raw beets, cut into roughly ½ in (1 cm) slices
1 yellow zucchini, cut into roughly ½ in (1 cm) slices
1 green zucchini, cut into roughly ½ in (1 cm) slices
2 red onions, cut into roughly ½ in (1 cm) slices
⅔ cup (150g) Tomato & Olive Sauce (see p14)
1 egg, lightly beaten
salt and freshly ground black pepper

YOU WILL NEED
large baking sheet, 15 x 10½ in (38 x 27 cm), lined with parchment paper

1 Preheat the oven to 375°F (180°C). Unroll the pastry and set aside.

2 Mark out a large rectangle on the parchment paper, the same size as the pastry, and place it drawn-side down on the baking sheet. Drizzle generously with half of the olive oil and dot all over with small pieces of butter. Sprinkle with the oregano, thyme, and rosemary, followed by a dusting of paprika. Scatter over the lemon zest.

3 Leaving a ½ in (2 cm) border, arrange the vegetables in four overlapping rows within the drawn rectangle on the parchment paper. Each row should butt up against the next one, without overlapping. (You can arrange the vegetables randomly or in groups, depending on your preference.) Season with salt and pepper, and drizzle over the remaining olive oil.

4 Carefully spoon the tomato and olive sauce over—little dollops of sauce spread with the back of a spoon will help to ensure you don't move the rows of vegetables.

5 Drape the pastry carefully over the sauce-topped vegetables. Using the back of a fork or teaspoon, press around the edges of the pastry to seal. Score the top in a diamond pattern with a sharp knife and then brush with egg.

6 Bake for 40 minutes, or until the pastry is golden and crisp. Remove the tart from the oven and let it sit on the baking sheet for 10 minutes. Lay a piece of parchment paper on top, followed by a cutting board, and carefully flip the tart over in one swift move. Remove the baking sheet and peel off the backing paper. Scatter over a few oregano leaves and cut into portions to serve.

Mushroom & Leek Monkey Crust Pie

Fall is all about warming, comfort food. And this pie is the king of comfort—with its filling of wild mushrooms, woody herbs, and leeks it's a celebration of the season. The monkey crust pie topping is perfect for using up any leftover bits of pastry you may have lingering in the fridge or freezer.

Serves 4

1 tbsp olive oil
3 tbsp (50g) salted butter
3 shallots, chopped
1 large leek, chopped
12oz (350g) mixed wild
   mushrooms, sliced
1 tsp chopped rosemary leaves
1 tsp chopped thyme leaves
1 tbsp chopped chives
4 premade 9¾ x 10½ in
   sheets of puff pastry or use
   homemade (see p12) rolled
   to two 14 x 9in (35 x 23 cm)
   rounds
1 egg, lightly beaten
steamed vegetables, to serve
   (optional)

For the creamy mustard sauce:

2 cups (500ml) whole milk
⅓ cup (50g) all-purpose flour
3 tbsp (50g) salted butter
2 tbsp white wine
3½oz (100g) aged Gouda
   cheese, finely grated
1 tsp Dijon mustard
salt and freshly ground
   black pepper

YOU WILL NEED

8 in (20 cm) round pie dish,
   greased with butter

1 Preheat the oven to 375°F (190°C).

2 To make the creamy mustard sauce, pour the milk into a saucepan on medium heat, then add the flour and butter. Using a balloon whisk, gently whisk the sauce for about 3 minutes, until it begins to thicken. Stir in the white wine and continue to cook, whisking, for another 3 minutes. Turn the heat to its lowest setting and cook the sauce for a further 5 minutes, whisking occasionally, to prevent it catching on the bottom, until thick and creamy. Take the pan off the heat and stir the Gouda cheese and mustard into the sauce. Season with a little salt and pepper, to taste, then set aside.

3 Heat the olive oil and butter in a large sauté pan on medium heat. Add the shallots and sauté for 3 minutes, or until they start to soften. Stir in the leek and sauté gently for another 5 minutes, until softened. Add the mushrooms and herbs to the pan, stir, cover with the lid, and cook for 6 minutes. The mushrooms should release their liquid and soften. Remove the lid, turn the heat up a little, season with salt and plenty of pepper, and sauté until the mushrooms take on a golden color and the liquid has evaporated. Pour the creamy mustard sauce into the pan and stir until combined. Leave the sauce to cool while you prepare the crust.

4 Unroll a pastry sheet and place it in the greased pie dish. Trim the edges, ensuring you leave a ¾ in (2 cm) overhang, then brush the edge with water. Pour in the cooled, creamy leek and mushroom filling.

5 Unroll (or roll out) the remaining pastry and cut it into small squares, each roughly 2 x 2 in (5 x 5 cm). Randomly arrange the squares over the filling until the top of the pie is covered. Crimp the edge of the pie to join the top and base. Brush with egg and bake for 40 minutes, or until the pastry is golden and crisp. Cut into slices and serve with steamed vegetables, if you like.

Upside Down Banana PB&J

The first time I had a toasted sandwich made in a proper sandwich toaster was in the early '80s, and I was at my friend Gabby's house. Her mum made a peanut butter and jam sandwich, and I think my mind melted with excitement. My upside-down version is more of a naughty midnight feast than something you'd eat for lunch or dinner, but it's well worth turning the oven on for!

Serves 2

2 premade 9¾ x 10½ in
    sheets of puff pastry or use
    homemade (see p12) rolled
    to 14 x 9in (35 x 23 cm)
4 tbsp peanut butter, crunchy
    or smooth
3 tbsp honey
2½oz (75g) raspberries
2½oz (75g) blueberries
1 banana, cut into slices
1 egg, lightly beaten

YOU WILL NEED
large baking sheet, roughly
    15 x 10½in (38 x 27 cm),
    lined with parchment paper

1 Preheat the oven to 425°F (220°C). Unroll the pastry and cut out two 5½in (14 cm) squares. Spread 2 tablespoons of the peanut butter over each square, leaving a narrow border. Place in the fridge until needed.

2 Mark out 2 squares on the parchment paper, the same size as the pastry and with space between each one, and place drawn-side down on the baking sheet. Drizzle the honey over the marked squares.

3 Arrange the raspberries and blueberries on top of one of the squares, leaving a ½in (1 cm) border. Place the banana slices on the second pastry square, leaving a narrow border.

4 Lay a square of puff pastry, peanut butter-side down, over each pile of fruit. Using the back of a teaspoon, scallop the edges of each pastry square to seal. Score the tops in a diamond pattern with a sharp knife and then brush with egg.

5 Bake for 25 minutes, until the pastry is golden and crisp. Remove the tarts from the oven and let them sit on the baking sheet for 5 minutes. Lay a piece of parchment paper on top, followed by a cutting board, and carefully flip the tarts over in one swift move. Remove the baking sheet and peel off the backing paper. Allow to cool for a further 5 minutes.

6 Slide a spatula underneath one of the squares and flip it over on top of the second square to make the ultimate BPB&J! Slice diagonally in half to serve.

Dinner Party Feasts

I remained in London while at university, and spent the first year living at home with Mum. I'm not sure if she was expecting typical student behavior from me—staggering home drunk at 3:00 a.m. or holding banging house parties in the garage—but she certainly didn't get that. Instead, I spent evenings hosting dinner parties for my eclectic art foundation friends. Yes, there was a lot of wine, and while there may have been a pile of dishes left in the sink, and a pile of sleeping bodies on sofas in the morning, it was all very well behaved. The food was often experimental, but there was always a lot of it: three proper courses with sides, and cocktails, and wine. It was all very suburban sitcom but delightful and civilized, and it's what I like to do to this day. In this chapter, I'm sharing three dinner party menus that will keep everyone happy, including a traditional Jewish Friday night dinner.

Friday Night Dinner

*Chopped Liver with Poppy & Fennel Seed Crackers • Roast Chicken •
Upside Down Cauliflower Cheese Tart • Chocolate Chestnut Roulade*

Growing up, Friday night dinners were always a big deal at our house. While Mum
was keen to encourage my brother and I to take an active interest in religion, we
were there for the food. And the food was good. Mum always cooked the classics:
a starter of chopped liver, followed by roast chicken with all the trimmings, usually
cauliflower and cheese, and finishing off with some kind of dessert, often served
with a fruit salad. I've recreated it here with a few upside-down twists.

Chopped Liver with Poppy & Fennel Seed Crackers
SERVES 4–6 (AS A CANAPÉ OR STARTER)

With all the reverence this dish carries in the
Jewish community, you'd have thought it was
complicated to make or included rare ingredients.
Yet it's unbelievably simple, if not downright basic.
It would originally have been made with schmaltz
(rendered chicken or goose fat) but unless you've
recently roasted a bird, I think it's a step too far.
I prefer a combination of olive oil and butter.

3 large free-range eggs
3 tbsp (50g) salted butter
1 tbsp olive oil
1 white onion, finely chopped
14oz (400g) chicken livers, veiny bits trimmed,
  if preferred
salt and freshly ground
  black pepper
Poppy & Fennel Seed Crackers (see p51) or
  toast, or your choice of crackers, to serve

1 Hard-boil the eggs in a small saucepan of
   boiling water for 10 minutes, then peel and
   set aside to cool.

2 Heat the butter and oil in a large, shallow
   skillet on medium heat. Once the butter
   has melted, add the onion and sauté gently
   until soft and just beginning to color.

3 Turn the heat up to medium–high, add
   the livers to the pan and fry, stirring
   occasionally, for about 8 minutes, until
   cooked with a touch of pink in the middle.
   (Many people cook their livers all the way
   through, which is also fine; the pâté will just
   be a bit drier and coarser.) Season with
   plenty of salt and pepper—the livers can
   take it! Set aside to cool slightly.

4 Cut the eggs in half and set aside one half
   of an egg, then add the remaining eggs and
   cooked liver mixture to a food processor and
   blitz until finely chopped. You don't want it
   to be too smooth. Transfer the mixture to a
   shallow serving dish and grate the remaining
   egg over the top.

5 Place the pâté in the fridge to settle for at
   least 1 hour, or it can be made up to 1 day in
   advance and stored in an airtight container
   in the fridge. Serve with Poppy & Fennel
   Seed Crackers.

Roast Chicken
MAIN (SERVES 4)

It may seem odd to include a recipe for such a classic, but sometimes they are the ones most often forgotten, or at least set aside for new, trendy dishes. This is a classic for good reason—Friday night dinner roast chicken is the best. You'd better agree, or my mum will come for you! Serve it with all your favorite sides and trimmings.

3lb 3oz (1.5kg) free-range chicken
1 large onion, sliced into wedges
2 celery sticks, chopped
1 carrot, chopped
3 garlic cloves, left whole
   and unpeeled
few sprigs each of rosemary and/or thyme
⅔ cup (150ml) white wine
salt and freshly ground
   black pepper

For the herb butter:
6 tbsp (100g) salted butter, softened
1 tsp chopped rosemary
1 tsp chopped thyme

YOU WILL NEED
large roasting pan

1 Preheat the oven to 350°F (180°C). To prepare the chicken (and for the ultimate crispy skin), place the bird in a large bowl in the sink. Pour over enough just-boiled water from a kettle to cover, then leave the chicken for a few minutes while you prepare the vegetables.

2 Spread half of the onion wedges along with all the celery, carrot, and garlic over the bottom of the roasting pan. Carefully lift the chicken out of the hot water and lay it on top of the vegetables, breast-side up. Stuff the rest of the onion inside the cavity along with the rosemary and/or thyme sprigs.

3 To make the herb butter, mix all the ingredients in a bowl until combined. Slide your fingers gently under the chicken skin to separate it from the breast. Take half of the herb butter and push it under the skin in an even layer, then spread the rest over the top of the chicken.

4 Turn the chicken over so it's breast-side-down. Season the bottom of the chicken with salt and pepper and pour the white wine into the tin. Place the chicken in the oven and roast for 1 hour, then remove from the oven.

5 Increase the oven temperature to 400°F (200°C). Using two forks, turn the chicken over, breast-side-up, and pop it back in the oven for a final 30–45 minutes, or until the skin is golden brown. To check the chicken is cooked, gently pull one leg away from the body and puncture the flesh in the crevice between the leg and the breast–the juices should run clear. If it's cloudy or a little bloody, then put the chicken back in the oven for a few minutes.

6 Once the chicken is out of the oven, cover it with foil and a dish towel and set it aside to rest, while the cauliflower cheese tart bakes (see p113).

Cook's Note:
I always buy a medium-sized chicken, no matter how many people I'm cooking for (a medium bird will feed 4 people with nothing left on the bones). If you have more than 4 guests (or want leftovers), I recommend buying 2 medium chickens and roasting them side-by-side in a large roasting pan (this is so much nicer than buying a larger bird). Leftover, cooked chicken will keep for up to 3 days in the fridge.

Upside Down Cauliflower Cheese Tart

SIDE (SERVES 4–6)

Cauliflower cheese was my mum's go-to side dish. It wouldn't be a Friday night dinner without it. This version uses all the classic components but in a delicious tart form.

2 premade 9¾ x 10½ in sheets of puff pastry
   or use homemade (see p12) rolled to
   14 x 9in (35 x 23 cm)
1 tbsp Dijon mustard
drizzle of olive oil
1 tsp thyme leaves
1 cup (100g) breadcrumbs
3½oz (100g) sharp Cheddar cheese, grated
1 cauliflower, leaves removed, cut into
   small florets
scant cup (200ml) Cheese Sauce (made with
   Cheddar, see p14), left to cool slightly
1 egg, lightly beaten
salt and freshly ground black pepper
few small sprigs of rosemary, to garnish

YOU WILL NEED

large baking sheet, roughly 15 x 10½ in
   (38 x 27 cm), lined with parchment paper

1 While the chicken is roasting in the oven, unroll the pastry and spread the mustard over one side, leaving a narrow border. Place in the fridge until needed.

2 Mark out a large rectangle on the parchment paper, the same size as the pastry, and place it drawn-side down on the baking sheet. Drizzle generously with olive oil and sprinkle with the thyme. Season with salt and pepper.

3 Leaving a ½ in (1 cm) border, sprinkle the breadcrumbs over the seasoned oil on the marked rectangle, followed by the grated Cheddar. Arrange the cauliflower florets on top in an even layer, then pour the slightly cooled cheese sauce over.

4 Lay the pastry, mustard-side down, over the cauliflower cheese. Using the back of a teaspoon, scallop the edges of the pastry to seal. Score the top in a diamond pattern with a sharp knife and then brush with beaten egg.

5 Bake at 400°F (200°C) for 25–30 minutes, until the pastry is golden and crisp. Remove the tart from the oven and let it sit on the baking sheet for 5 minutes. Lay a piece of parchment paper on top of the pie, followed by a cutting board, and carefully flip it over. Remove the baking sheet and peel off the backing paper. Slice into squares and scatter over a few sprigs of rosemary. Serve with the roast chicken, sides, and trimmings of your choice.

Chocolate Chestnut Roulade
DESSERT (SERVES 4 WITH LEFTOVERS)

A roulade may be considered a tricky option when it comes to dinner-party desserts, but Mum's version is pretty much fail-safe, partly because it's supposed to look crumbly, cracked, and messy! I realize, as I write, that this could have been what she told us to save face, but either way, I love the way it looks, and it reminds me of Mum, and that's the most important thing.

For the sponge:
4 large eggs, separated
½ cup plus 2 tbsp (125g) sugar
5½oz (150g) good-quality plain chocolate
   (at least 75% cocoa solids), broken
   into even-sized pieces
1½ tbsp hot water

For the filling:
1¼ cup (300ml) whipping cream
1 cup (250g) sweet chestnut spread
   or chocolate hazelnut spread

YOU WILL NEED
large 13½ x 9½ in (34 x 24 cm) jelly roll pan,
   lined with foil or parchment paper, greased
   well with butter

1 Preheat the oven to 340°F (170°C). In a large bowl, beat the egg yolks with the sugar until pale and creamy.

2 Melt the chocolate (I do this gradually in a microwave or use the classic heatproof bowl set over a pan of simmering water method). When melted, add the hot water, then gently stir the melted chocolate into the egg and sugar mixture.

3 Using an electric hand whisk, beat the egg whites to stiff peaks and then gently fold them into the chocolate mixture. Pour it into the lined pan, spreading it out evenly to cover the base. Bake for 20 minutes, then reduce the temperature to 200°F (120°C) and bake the sponge for a further 10 minutes, until risen and springy.

4 Meanwhile, grease another sheet of foil or parchment paper, slightly larger than the jelly roll pan, and place it on a flat surface or large board where it won't need to be moved for a while (around 8 hours).

5 Now the tricky bit. When the sponge is ready, take the pan out of the oven and immediately turn it over onto the greased foil/paper. Leave the sponge, with the pan still on top, for at least 8 hours. I tend to bake it in the morning, then get on with life, or bake it in the evening and let it sit overnight.

6 To make the filling/topping, whip the cream to a soft, light, whippy consistency in a large bowl. Gently fold in the chestnut or hazelnut spread until combined.

7 Remove the pan covering the sponge and carefully peel off the foil/paper backing. Spread the cream mixture evenly over the sponge. Starting at one of the short ends, using the foil/paper to help you, roll the sponge into a roulade—don't worry about any cracks or breaks, this is all part of the look. Carefully place the roulade on a serving plate and cut into slices to serve.

*Upside Down Smoked Mackerel & Tomato Tart • Slow Roasted Lamb with
Herby Potatoes and Vegetables • Upside Down Carrot, Honey & Thyme Tarte Tatin •
Build-your-own Summer Berry Trifle Cocktails*

When I'm entertaining my friends, I want there to be an abundance of food, but
I also want the meal to be easy. I'd rather spend time with them than be stuck in the
kitchen. All the dishes in this menu look after themselves, by which I mean there's
very little prep, and they're supposed to be served family style at the table, so
everyone can just dig in.

Upside Down Smoked Mackerel & Tomato Tart

SERVES 4–6

The combo of smoky mackerel with sun-dried
tomato cream cheese makes the perfect filling for
this puff pastry tart. I love the idea of placing it
upside down in the center of the table, and once
everyone takes their seats, flipping it over to do
the big reveal, and then letting everyone tear in.
Like a proper bacchanalian feast!

2 premade 9¾ x 10½ in sheets of puff pastry
 or use homemade (see p12) rolled to
 14 x 9in (35 x 23 cm)
7oz (200g) cream cheese
3½oz (100g) smoked sun-dried tomatoes in oil,
 drained, reserving 1 tbsp of the oil
drizzle of olive oil
1 tbsp roughly chopped dill
3 smoked mackerel fillets, skin removed, and
 portioned into 9 bite-sized pieces
1 egg, lightly beaten
salt and freshly ground black pepper

YOU WILL NEED
large baking sheet, roughly 15 x 10½ in
 (38 x 27 cm), lined with parchment paper

1 Preheat the oven to 425°F (220°C). Unroll
   the pastry and set aside until needed.

2 Place the cream cheese and sun-dried
   tomatoes with their oil in a food processor,
   then blitz until smooth. Set aside.

3 Drizzle the lined baking sheet generously
   with olive oil and sprinkle with the dill.
   Season with salt and pepper.

4 Arrange the smoked mackerel pieces evenly
   spaced apart on the lined baking sheet (3
   rows of 3). Top the mackerel with a teaspoon
   of the cream cheese mixture.

5 Carefully drape the pastry over the cream
   cheese–topped mackerel. Press the pastry
   down between the pieces of mackerel until
   you can see nine defined mounds of fish, then
   seal in the filling with a fork. Press around
   the edges of the whole pastry sheet to seal.
   Score the top in a diamond pattern with a
   sharp knife and then brush with egg.

6 Bake for 25–30 minutes, until the pastry is
   golden and crisp. Remove the tart from the
   oven and let it sit on the baking sheet for 5
   minutes. Lay a piece of parchment paper on
   top, followed by a cutting board, and carefully
   flip it over. Remove the baking sheet and peel
   off the backing paper. When ready to serve (it
   can be served hot or cold), let your guests to
   pull the tart apart or slice into portions.

Slow-Roasted Lamb with Herby Potatoes and Vegetables
MAIN (SERVES 4–6)

Last summer, while on the glorious island of Mallorca, we were invited to our friend's place for lunch. Antonia and Pepe are true Mallorquins, proud of their wonderful home and all that the island produces. Pepe cooked us what I can only describe as the best roast lamb I've ever eaten. Slow roasted, along with potatoes, garlic, and rosemary, in their traditional outdoor oven; it couldn't have been simpler or more delicious, and he very kindly gave me his recipe so that I can share it with you. Cooked until falling off the bone, the lamb must be eaten to be believed—a true feast for friends.

4 potatoes, such as Yukon Gold, cut into
   bite-sized chunks
3 carrots, cut into bite-sized chunks
5 shallots, quartered
9oz (250g) vine cherry tomatoes
3–4 garlic cloves, depending on size,
   left whole
drizzle of olive oil
3 rosemary sprigs
4lb (1.85kg) half leg of lamb
1¼ cup (300ml) white wine

For the rub:
1 garlic clove, peeled
2 tsp chopped rosemary leaves
2 tsp chopped thyme leaves
1 tsp dried oregano
splash of olive oil
salt and freshly ground black pepper

YOU WILL NEED
large roasting pan with tight-fitting
   lid or foil

1. Preheat the oven to 425°F (220°C). Start with the rub. Blitz the garlic with the herbs and a splash of olive oil in a mini food processor to a chunky paste. Season with salt and pepper. Set aside.

2. Put the potatoes, carrots, shallots, tomatoes, and whole garlic cloves in a large roasting pan, drizzle over a little olive oil, and place the rosemary sprigs and leg of lamb on top. Rub the lamb all over with the garlic rub, then roast in the oven for 30 minutes, until browned all over.

3. Carefully remove the pan from the oven, pour the white wine over the lamb and vegetables and put the lid on, making sure it's tight-fitting (or cover with foil—I use both). Reduce the heat to 350°F (180°C). Place the roasting pan back in the oven and cook for 4½ hours.

4. At this point, remove the lid/foil and turn the oven back up to 425°F (220°C) for a final 20-minute blast. By now, the lamb should be starting to fall off the bone with crispy bits around the edges, and the vegetables and garlic gloriously soft and golden. Remove the pan from the oven.

5. Using 2 forks, shred the roast lamb off the bone in chunks. Serve the shredded lamb on top of the roasted vegetables and garlic with the lamb juices spooned over.

Upside Down Carrot, Honey & Thyme Tarte Tatin
SIDE (SERVES 4–6)

Honey-glazed carrots go beautifully with roasted meats, especially lamb, and work well as a topping in this savory puff pastry tarte tartin. It takes a little effort to arrange the carrots, but it's worth it for the finished result.

2 premade 9¾ x 10½ in sheets of puff pastry
   or use homemade (see p12) rolled to
   14 x 9 in (35 x 23 cm)
2 tbsp chile jam
drizzle of olive oil
drizzle of honey, plus extra to serve
5 tbsp (75g) salted butter, cut into small pieces
2 thyme sprigs, leaves picked
4 large carrots, cut into rounds no thicker
   than a thick coin
1 egg, lightly beaten
salt and freshly ground black pepper

YOU WILL NEED
large baking sheet, roughly 15 x 10½ in
   (38 x 27 cm), lined with parchment paper
8½ in (22 cm) diameter round plate

1 Preheat the oven to 400°F (200°C). Unroll the pastry. Using the 8½ in (22 cm) round plate as a template, cut the pastry into a disk. Slather the chile jam over one side of the pastry, leaving a narrow border. Place in the fridge until needed.

2 Draw around the same plate onto the parchment paper, then place it drawn-side down on the baking sheet. Drizzle a little olive oil and honey over the marked round, then dot the butter on top. Finish with a sprinkling of thyme, saving some to serve, and season with salt and pepper.

3 Place one large carrot round in the center of the parchment paper circle, then working your way outward, place the carrot slices in overlapping rings around the central slice. Start with the larger rounds in the center, making sure you leave a ¾ in (2 cm) border around the outer edge—you should have at least 5 rings of overlapping carrot slices. Season with extra salt and pepper.

4 Lay the pastry disk over the top of the carrots. Using the back of a fork, press around the edge of the pastry to seal. Score the top in a diamond pattern with a sharp knife and then brush with egg.

5 Bake for 30 minutes, or until the pastry is golden and crisp. Remove the tart from the oven and allow it to sit on the baking sheet for 5 minutes. Lay a piece of parchment paper on top, followed by a cutting board or plate, and carefully flip it over. Remove the baking sheet and peel off the backing paper. Finish with a sprinkling of the reserved thyme and a drizzle of honey. Serve cut into slices as a side to the roasted lamb, potatoes, and vegetables.

Build-Your-Own Summer Berry Trifle Cocktails
DESSERT (SERVES 6)

I love the idea of placing the various elements of this trifle on the table, and allowing guests to build their own dessert. All the essential ingredients are here, plus a selection of spirits and cordials so people can go as boozy (or not) as they like. I've cheated and used ready-made custard and cake, but if you have the time and inclination, feel free to make your own. I've also used summer berries, but you can use any seasonal fruit your heart desires.

1¼ cup (300ml) whipping cream
7oz (200g) vanilla sponge cake, cut into
    small cubes
selection of alcohol, such as sherry, amaro,
    or flavored vodka
selection of fruit cordials, diluted with
    water, to taste
selection of jams
1¼ cup (300ml) cold vanilla custard
7oz (200g) blueberries
7oz (200g) raspberries
7oz (200g) strawberries, halved or
    quartered, if large
7oz (200g) blackberries
6 cherries (optional)

YOU WILL NEED
6 classic parfait glasses, or
    clear glass bowls (it's nice to
    be able to see the layers of trifle)

1 Using an electric hand whisk, whip the cream in a large bowl to soft, light peaks. Place the bowl on your dining table or worktop with all the other ingredients listed in separate bottles and bowls. You'll also need plenty of spoons.

2 Let your guests build their own trifles: I would suggest starting with a few cubes of cake and a splash or two of liquid (alcoholic or diluted cordial) to let it soak into the cake. Add a layer of jam, custard, and fruit—choose your own favorite combinations.

3 Finish each trifle with a generous topping of softly whipped cream, then pop a cherry on top, if you like. Enjoy!

If Tarts Be the Food of Love

Salt & Pepper Bang Bang Cauliflower Love Bites • Upside Down "Marry Me" Chicken Tart with Roasted Garlic & Parmesan Greens • Upside Down Banana & Custard Tart

When I first met my husband (The Viking), I wanted to impress him with my cooking skills, but little did I know what I was taking on. It's not that he's a fussy eater, but he likes what he likes, and has an innate inability to try something new. I thought a twist on duck à l'orange (he wasn't vegetarian at the time) would be an impressive first meal. Let's just say that it didn't go down too well. Since then, we don't do romantic meals, but if we did, this small feast would be on the menu.

Salt & Pepper Bang Bang Cauliflower Love Bites
STARTER (SERVES 2)

Irresistible as part of a cheekily romantic meal for two, these cauliflower bites are both delicious and fun to eat, especially if you serve them to each other dipped in something sweet and saucy. You can cook them in an air fryer or the oven.

⅔ cup (90g) all-purpose flour
¾ cup (175ml) half milk/half Greek yogurt,
    stirred well
½ tbsp sea salt flakes
4 tsp freshly ground black pepper, plus
    extra to season
1 tbsp finely grated unwaxed lemon zest
1½ cups (150g) breadcrumbs
1 cauliflower, chopped into bite-sized
    chunks/florets
1 tbsp finely chopped chives

For the bang bang glaze:
juice of 3 unwaxed lemons
3 tbsp honey
1 tbsp soy sauce
1 tsp cornstarch mixed with 1 tsp water

YOU WILL NEED
large baking sheet, roughly 15 x 10½ in
    (38 x 27 cm), lined with parchment paper
    (if using the oven and not an air fryer)

1   Preheat your air fryer to 350°F (180°C) or oven to 400°F (200°C).

2   Using a balloon whisk, mix the flour, milk/yogurt, salt, 3 teaspoons of the black pepper, and the lemon zest in a large bowl to make a batter. Add the breadcrumbs to a second large bowl.

3   Add the cauliflower to the batter mixture and use a spoon to turn it until coated. Transfer the cauliflower to the breadcrumbs and turn to coat each piece in the crumbs.

4   Cook in the air fryer for 15 minutes, or place on the lined baking sheet and bake in the oven for 25 minutes, until golden and crisp.

5   Meanwhile, make the glaze. Warm all the ingredients in a small pan with the remaining black pepper, stirring until thick and glossy.

6   When the cauliflower bites are ready, toss them in the glaze, then return them to the air fryer or oven for a final 5 minutes, until glossy and sticky. Sprinkle over the chives and serve.

Upside Down "Marry Me" Chicken Tart with Roasted Garlic & Parmesan Greens
MAIN (SERVES 2 WITH LEFTOVERS)

"Marry Me" chicken was an internet sensation; the idea behind the dish is that it's so good it could lead to a marriage proposal! Both impressive and ridiculously easy to make, this upside-down tart is a play on the original.

2 premade 9¾ x 10½ in sheets of puff pastry
   or use homemade (see p12) rolled to
   14 x 9 in (35 x 23 cm)
5 asparagus stalks, each cut in half
drizzle of olive oil
1 tsp dried oregano
½ tsp chile flakes
7 oz (200g) leftover roast chicken, shredded
1 egg, lightly beaten

For the "Marry Me" sauce:
1 cup (250ml) milk of choice
3 tbsp (25g) all-purpose flour
2 tbsp (30g) lightly salted butter
1 garlic clove, crushed
1½ tsp sun-dried tomato paste
¾ cup (75g) Parmesan cheese, finely grated
3 tbsp heavy cream
salt and freshly ground black pepper

For the roasted greens:
7 oz (200g) green beans
7 oz (200g) broccolini
2 garlic cloves, grated
2 tbsp olive oil
1¼ cup (150g) Parmesan cheese, finely grated

YOU WILL NEED
large baking sheet, roughly 15 x 10½ in
   (38 x 27 cm), lined with parchment paper
large roasting pan

1 Start with the sauce. Warm the milk in a pan over medium heat, then add the flour and butter. Using a balloon whisk, whisk the sauce for 6 minutes, until creamy and thick. Add the garlic, turn the heat to its lowest setting and cook the sauce for a further 5 minutes, whisking every so often to ensure it doesn't catch on the bottom. Season with a little salt and pepper, to taste, then stir in the sun-dried tomato paste, Parmesan cheese, and finally the cream. Set aside until needed.

2 Preheat the oven to 425°F (220°C). Unroll the pastry and set aside.

3 Blanch the asparagus in a small pan of boiling water for 3 minutes, then drain and refresh in cold water. Drain again and set aside.

4 Mark out a large rectangle on the parchment paper, the same size as the pastry, and place it drawn-side down on the baking sheet. Drizzle with a little olive oil, then sprinkle over the oregano and chile flakes. Season with salt and pepper.

5 Leaving a ¾ in (2 cm) border, place the chicken on top of the seasoned oil, then add the asparagus. Season with more salt and pepper. Carefully pour the sauce over.

6 Drape the pastry over the top of the saucy chicken and asparagus. Using the back of a teaspoon, scallop the edges of the pastry to seal. Score the top in a diamond pattern with a sharp knife and then brush with egg.

7 Bake for 35 minutes, or until the pastry is golden and crisp. Remove the tart from the oven and let it sit on the baking sheet for 5 minutes. Lay a piece of parchment paper on top, followed by a cutting board, and carefully flip the tart over. Remove the baking sheet and peel off the backing paper. (You may want to slide the tart back onto the baking sheet and into the oven for a few minutes to get a little more golden on top before serving.)

8 Meanwhile, roast the greens. Place the vegetables and garlic in a large roasting pan. Drizzle over the olive oil, add half of the Parmesan cheese and mix well. Cook at the same time as the tart for 15–20 minutes, until tender and golden. Sprinkle the remaining Parmesan cheese over the greens, then serve with the tart.

Upside Down Banana
& Custard Tart
DESSERT (SERVES 2 WITH LEFTOVERS)

I asked The Viking what he would love to have for dessert if I were to make him a romantic meal, and his answer was "bananas and custard." I guess his palate is on brand with my kind of cooking: simple, homey, classic, and reminiscent of the foods we both loved in childhood. So, I made his suggestion into a tart with the golden, crisp pastry a bonus!

2 premade 9¾ x 10½ in sheets of puff pastry
   or use homemade (see p12) rolled to
   14 x 9 in (35 x 23 cm)
drizzle of honey
2 bananas (slightly underripe is best),
   thickly sliced
1 egg, lightly beaten
powdered sugar, for dusting
heavy cream, to serve

For the custard:
¾ cup (175ml) whole milk
3 large egg yolks
¾oz (20g) sugar
1 tsp grated nutmeg, plus a little extra
   for sprinkling
½ tsp vanilla extract

YOU WILL NEED
large baking sheet, roughly 15 x 10½ in
   (38 x 27 cm), lined with parchment paper
8½ in (22 cm) diameter round plate

1. Start with the custard. Warm the milk in a pan over medium heat until it starts to lightly simmer; do not let it boil. Remove the pan from the heat.

2. Place the egg yolks and sugar in a large bowl and whisk until pale and creamy. Slowly pour the warm milk over the egg yolks, whisking with a balloon whisk. Stir in the nutmeg and vanilla. Pour the custard mixture into a large bowl and set aside to cool.

3. Preheat the oven to 425°F (220°C). Unroll the pastry. Using the 8½ in (22 cm) round plate as a template, cut the pastry into a disk. Place in the fridge until needed.

4. Draw around the same plate onto the parchment paper, then place it drawn-side down on the baking sheet. Drizzle honey over the marked round and sprinkle with a little grated nutmeg.

5. Leaving a ¾ in (2 cm) border, lay the banana slices in two circles on top of the marked round (you need to create a circular ring or barrier of bananas). Now pour the custard into the middle and tuck any remaining banana slices into the custard.

6. Lay the pastry disk on top of the bananas and custard. Using the back of a teaspoon, scallop the edge of the pastry to seal. Score the top in a diamond pattern with a sharp knife and then brush with egg.

7. Bake for 30 minutes, or until the pastry is golden and crisp. Remove the tart from the oven and let it sit on the baking sheet for 10 minutes. Lay a piece of parchment paper, then a cutting board or plate on top and carefully flip the tart over. Remove the baking sheet and peel off the backing paper. Dust the top of the tart with powdered sugar and serve cut into slices with cream on the side.

Sweet Celeb

ations

A feast wouldn't be a feast without a sweet conclusion, and this chapter is the ultimate in spoil-yourself treats and fun creations. From an upside-down birthday cake and twist on the traditional cream tea through to desserts for special occasions and festivities—including Halloween, Valentine's Day, and Easter—these sweet centerpieces will take you on a celebratory journey through the year. If you're wondering why there are no Christmas recipes, for me, this festive highlight deserves its very own chapter (see pp158–81).

Apple Tarte Tatin

The start of the year coincides with the beginning of my "upside-down" journey... perhaps I wouldn't be here today if it weren't for this classic apple tart, the origins of which really speak to me. The story revolves around the Tatin sisters, Stéphanie and Caroline, who ran the Hôtel Tatin in Lamotte-Beuvron, France. One day, Chef Stéphanie accidentally caramelized some apples for too long. To salvage the dessert, she placed a sheet of pastry on top of the fruit, then baked it, flipping the tart over to serve to guests. They loved it, and the tarte tatin was born. This is my version, the perfect comforting dessert to brighten an often dull January.

Serves 4

1 recipe quantity of Shortcrust
  Pie Dough (see p12) rolled to
  roughly 14 x 9 in (35 x 23 cm)
1½ cups (300g) sugar
1 tsp vanilla extract
6 tbsp (100g) salted butter,
  cut into cubes
8 apples (I like to use a
  sharp-sweet apple, like
  a Granny Smith) peeled,
  cored, and quartered
vanilla ice cream, to serve

YOU WILL NEED

7 in (18 cm) diameter heavy
  cast-iron, ovenproof skillet

1 Preheat the oven to 375°F (190°C). Unroll the pastry and cut a round roughly ¾ in (2 cm) larger than the diameter of the skillet. Place in the fridge until needed.

2 Add the sugar and vanilla to the skillet and place it on medium heat. Let the sugar heat, without stirring, until melted and starting to form a caramel; this takes about 5 minutes. Carefully swirl the pan until any uncooked sugar is combined with the melted sugar. Do not stir. Cook for a further 5 minutes, or until the sugar melts and has turned into a dark, golden caramel. Carefully, take the pan off the heat.

3 Dot the cubes of butter over the caramel, then lay the apples in a single, even layer on top, packing them tightly into the pan. I like concentric rings of apples, but you can go freestyle here; it's up to you.

4 Once the base of the pan is covered in an even layer of apples, place the pastry round on top and tuck the edges in at the sides as much as you can.

5 Bake the tarte for 30 minutes, or until the pastry is crisp and golden. Remove the tarte from the oven and let it stand for 10 minutes (not longer—you must turn it out while still warm or the caramel will harden and stick to the pan). Place a platter or large plate on top of the pan and carefully flip it over. Lift off the pan and serve the tarte warm, cut into slices, with a large scoop of vanilla ice cream.

Valentine's Chocolate & Berry Lava Pie

Nothing says love like gooey chocolate. This foolproof lava cake is made in a large pie dish with the addition of raspberries, which are heavenly with chocolate. It also features a few fennel seeds, since The Viking loves the flavor of aniseed, and they add a touch of sophistication to the dessert. It's the perfect treat for Valentine's Day.

Serves 2 (with leftovers)

½ cup plus 3 tbsp (175g) salted butter
½ tsp fennel seeds (optional, but well worth it)
7oz (200g) 70% dark chocolate, chopped
3 large eggs
⅔ cup (125g) sugar
⅓ cup (40g) ground almonds or all-purpose flour
7oz (200g) raspberries
cream or ice cream, to serve

YOU WILL NEED
medium, rectangular baking dish, lightly greased with butter

1   Preheat the oven to 350°F (180°C).

2   Melt the butter with the fennel seeds, if using, in a saucepan on medium heat. Remove from the heat and gently stir through half of the chocolate until melted.

3   In a large bowl, whisk together the eggs and sugar using an electric hand whisk until pale and fluffy. Pour in the melted chocolate mixture, then sift in the ground almonds or flour. Gently stir in the raspberries and the remaining chocolate until everything is combined. Pour the mixture into the prepared pie dish.

4   Bake for 20 minutes, until the edge of the pie is firm and darkened, and the center is still slightly wobbly. Serve straightaway with cream or ice cream.

Upside Down Banoffee Pie

I love a portmanteau: word games, puns, and etymology are my favorite topics of conversation, so if I come across a name of a dish that is a play on words, then I'm a happy boy. Banoffee pie is one such dish, the name is a combination of banana and toffee, which coincidentally are two of my favorite things to eat. I've included all the classic banoffee elements in this upside-down version, but in a deconstructed way. It comes with a final flourish of whipped cream.

Serves 4–6

2 premade 9¾ x 10½ in sheets of puff pastry or use homemade (see p12) rolled to 14 x 9 in (35 x 23 cm)
3 tbsp (50g) salted butter, at room temperature
4 tbsp honey, plus extra for drizzling
2 tbsp sugar
4 graham crackers
3 just-ripe bananas, peeled and thickly sliced
1 egg, lightly beaten
1¼ cup (300ml) whipping cream
1¾oz (50g) dark chocolate, grated, to decorate

YOU WILL NEED
large baking sheet, roughly 15 x 10½ in (38 x 27 cm), lined with parchment paper
8½ in (22 cm) diameter round plate

1 Preheat the oven to 425°F (220°C). Unroll the pastry and cut out a round using the 8½ in (22 cm) diameter plate as a template. Place in the fridge until needed.

2 Draw around the same plate onto the parchment paper. Place the paper drawn-side down on the baking sheet.

3 Spread half of the butter within the drawn circle on the parchment paper, then drizzle over half of the honey and sprinkle with half of the sugar.

4 Leaving a ½ in (1 cm) border, crumble two of the cookies over the drawn circle and top with one of the sliced bananas. Repeat to create a second layer of butter, honey, sugar, cookies, and sliced banana.

5 Drape the pastry round over the top of the banana mixture. Using the back of a fork, press around the edge of the pastry to seal. Score the top in a diamond pattern with a sharp knife and then brush with egg.

6 Bake for 30 minutes, until the pastry is golden and crisp. Remove the pie from the oven and let it sit on the baking sheet for 10 minutes. Lay a piece of parchment paper on top, followed by a cutting board or plate and carefully flip it over. Remove the tray and peel off the backing paper, then let the pie cool.

7 Meanwhile, whip the cream to medium-soft peaks. Spoon the cream over the cooled tart and top with the remaining sliced banana, the grated chocolate, and an extra drizzle of honey.

Upside Down Carrot Cake

If I'm in a café or bakery, I almost always order carrot cake and I also love to make it at home. This is my go-to recipe, inspired by Delia Smith's ultimate carrot cake, which I've been baking, adapting, and enjoying for decades. It's the perfect cake for any celebrations you're planning.

Serves 8

For the cake:
¾ cup (175g), packed dark
 brown sugar
2 large eggs
⅔ cup (150ml) sunflower oil
1¼ cup (150g) all-purpose flour
1 tsp baking powder
½ tsp salt
½ cup (50g) ground almonds
1 tsp ground ginger
1 tsp ground cinnamon
1 tsp baking soda
7oz (200g) carrots, finely grated
grated zest of 1 orange
1 cup (110g) mixed dried fruit
 and candied peel
½ cup (50g) dried unsweetened
 coconut

For the topping:
¼ cup sugar
6 long, slim, heirloom carrots,
 halved lengthwise
small piece of salted butter
2 tbsp honey, plus extra to serve

For the cinnamon cream:
⅔ cup (150ml) whipping cream
3½oz (100g) cream cheese
1 tbsp powdered sugar
1 tsp ground cinnamon
finely grated zest of 1 orange

YOU WILL NEED
8in (20cm) round cake pan,
 lined with parchment paper

1   Preheat the oven to 375°F (190°C).

2   To make the topping, bring a pan of boiling water to a boil, stir in the sugar and add the carrots. Return the water to a boil, then turn the heat down to low and simmer for 10 minutes, or until the carrots are just tender. Drain well.

3   Spread a little butter over the lined base of the cake pan and drizzle with 1 tablespoon of the honey. Arrange the cooked carrots in the pan, cut-side down. Trim the carrots, if needed, so they fit tightly and neatly, then drizzle with the remaining honey.

4   To make the cake, whisk the sugar, eggs, and oil in a large bowl for 2–3 minutes using an electric hand whisk until smooth and creamy (a stand mixer would also work well here). Sift the flour, baking powder, salt, almonds, spices, and baking soda into the bowl, then whisk on a low speed until evenly combined. Fold in the rest of the cake ingredients and tip the mixture into the prepared cake pan on top of the candied carrots. Smooth the top with a palette knife.

5   Bake for 45 minutes, until the cake is golden and risen, and a skewer inserted into the middle comes out clean. Remove from the oven and leave the cake to cool in the pan on a wire rack.

6   Meanwhile, make the cinnamon cream. Whisk the cream to soft peaks in a large bowl, then add the cream cheese, powdered sugar, cinnamon, and orange zest and whisk again to firm peaks. Place in the fridge until needed.

7   Turn the cake out of the pan onto a serving plate or cake stand and remove the backing paper. Serve cut into slices with a large spoonful of the cinnamon cream. Finish with an extra drizzle of honey.

Pear & Pistachio Crinkle Cake

I love spring. The longer days, brighter skies, and the promise of summer around the corner, which really helps, as I have occasional bouts of anxiety during the darker, colder months. At times like this, I find baking incredibly therapeutic. A calming distraction. This cake is perfect for that—the folding of the pastry, the sprinkling of the nuts, and preparation of the fruit—plus, you're rewarded with a delicious bake at the end.

Serves 8

For the cake:

1¼ cup (150g) shelled, unsalted pistachios, plus extra to decorate

9oz (250g) pack of phyllo pastry (you need 10 sheets)

½ cup plus 2 tbsp (150g) salted butter, melted, plus extra for greasing

5 tbsp sugar, plus extra for sprinkling

2 just-ripe pears, halved lengthwise, core removed, and thinly sliced (no need to peel)

honey and Greek yogurt, to serve

For the custard:

1 cup (250ml) whole milk

½ tsp vanilla extract

1 cup (250ml) heavy cream

3 large eggs

1 large egg yolk

2 tbsp sugar

1 tbsp almond butter (or other nut butter or chocolate hazelnut spread)

YOU WILL NEED

8½ in (22 cm) round ovenproof dish, such as a flan dish or similar, greased

1   To make the custard, place the milk, vanilla, and cream in a small saucepan and gently heat to a simmer. Take the pan off the heat and let the mixture cool. You want it to be barely warm.

2   Crack the eggs into a large bowl. Add the extra yolk, sugar, and almond butter, and whisk with an electric hand whisk. Once combined, gradually pour in the warm milk in a steady stream, continuing to whisk on a low speed. Set aside once all the milk has been added.

3   Using the end of a rolling pin, or mini food processor in pulse mode, crush the pistachios to a rough crumble. Set aside.

4   Lay a sheet of phyllo pastry on your work surface and brush it with a little melted butter (this doesn't have to be perfectly done), then sprinkle with roughly 1 tablespoon of the crushed pistachios and ½ tablespoon of sugar. Pleat the sheet of phyllo like a fan into a 1½ in (4 cm) wide strip, or the same width as the depth of your dish, enclosing the pistachios and sugar within the folds. Place the strip of folded phyllo around the inside edge of the dish. Repeat with the remaining sheets of phyllo, pistachios, and sugar, arranging the strips in the dish in a circle, working from the outside inward in a fairly tight spiral, and slightly overlapping the edge of each pastry strip. Continue until you've used all the pastry sheets.

5   Preheat the oven to 375°F (190°C). Carefully press slices of pear between the folds of the phyllo pastry. Pour the custard over the top and sprinkle with extra sugar. Bake for 45 minutes, or until the top of the cake is golden and risen, and the custard has set.

6   To finish, drizzle the top with honey and sprinkle with extra crushed pistachios. Serve cut into slices with Greek yogurt.

Upside Down School Cake Tart

Kids of every generation love this cake (it was my favorite part of school dinners). The classic vanilla bake is topped with a simple icing and decorated with sprinkles. It's usually served cut into squares with loads of vanilla custard, but this version comes with an upside-down twist.

Serves 12

For the tart:
2 premade 9¾ x 10½ in sheets of puff pastry or use homemade (see p12) rolled to 14 x 9 in (35 x 23 cm)
2 tbsp seedless strawberry jam
drizzle of honey
2 tbsp candy sprinkles

For the cake:
½ cup plus 1 tbsp salted butter, softened, plus extra for greasing
¾ cup (140g) sugar
2 large eggs, lightly beaten
1 cup plus 1 tbsp (140g) all-purpose flour
1 tsp baking powder
½ tsp salt
1 tsp vanilla extract

For the icing:
7oz (200g) powdered sugar, sifted
candy sprinkles, to decorate
hot custard, to serve

YOU WILL NEED
large baking sheet, roughly 15 x 10½ in (38 x 27 cm), lined with parchment paper

1   Preheat the oven to 400°F (200°C). Unroll the pastry and spread a thin layer of jam over one side, leaving a ¾ in (2 cm) border. Place in the fridge until needed.

2   Mark out a large rectangle, the same size as the pastry, on the parchment paper and place it drawn-side down on the baking sheet. Drizzle the lined baking sheet with honey and lightly spread the sprinkles. Set aside.

3   To make the cake, cream the butter and sugar in a large bowl using an electric hand whisk until pale and fluffy. Add the eggs, flour, and vanilla and beat again to a smooth, thick cake batter. Pour the batter onto the lined baking sheet and spread it out evenly over the marked rectangle, leaving a ½ in (1 cm) border. It should be fairly thick and not run too much.

4   Carefully drape the pastry, jam-side down, over the cake batter. Using a teaspoon, scallop the edges of the pastry to seal. Score the top in a diamond pattern with a sharp knife and then brush with egg.

5   Bake for 35 minutes, or until the pastry is golden, and the cake is risen and cooked. Remove the tart from the oven and let it rest on the baking sheet for 10 minutes. Lay a piece of parchment paper on top, followed by a cutting board, and carefully flip it over. Remove the baking sheet and peel off the backing paper, then let cool.

6   To decorate the tart, mix the powdered sugar with enough water to make a thick icing. Spread the icing over the cooled cake, then decorate the top generously with sprinkles. Leave for about 1 hour, until the icing has set, then cut into squares and serve with hot custard.

Cream Cobbler

This takes the elements of a classic English afternoon treat—scone, strawberry jam, and thick clotted cream—and transforms them into a treat of a dessert. And you don't even have to worry about whether to top your scone with cream or jam first as everything is smooshed together in one delightful dish!

Serves 6

2⅓ cups (300g) all-purpose flour
2 tsp baking powder
1 tsp salt
6 tbsp (100g) cold lightly salted butter, cut into small cubes
½ cup (100g) sugar
1 egg, lightly beaten
4 tbsp whole milk or buttermilk
14oz (400g) strawberries, hulled, cut in half, if large, others left whole
1 cup (225g) clotted cream or crème fraîche
extra clotted cream, crème fraîche, or ice cream, to serve

YOU WILL NEED
8 in (20 cm) round ovenproof dish, base and sides greased

1 Preheat the oven to 400°F (200°C). Using your fingertips, rub the flour, baking powder, salt, and butter together in a large bowl to a breadcrumb consistency. Add the sugar, egg, and milk or buttermilk and, using a butter knife, bring everything together into a loose, shaggy dough.

2 Tip half of the strawberries into the ovenproof dish, followed by a few dollops of the clotted cream (about half). Add half of the cobbler dough on top of the strawberries in large spoonfuls. Repeat with the remaining strawberries, cream, and the cobbler dough. You don't have to be neat when assembling this dish—it should all be quite random.

3 Bake for 35–40 minutes, until the cobbler topping has risen and become golden. Remove from the oven and let cool slightly. Serve the cobbler with extra clotted cream, crème fraîche, or ice cream.

Plum & Chile Jam Galette

Plums, particularly Victoria plums, are my absolute favorite end-of-summer fruit. They remind me of my childhood: picking plums in the back garden at home, avoiding wasps, and getting bellyache from eating far too many. They cook beautifully, releasing so much juice and flavor, which is enhanced here by the spicy chile jam. This simple but elegant galette is the perfect way to celebrate the arrival of late summer fruit.

Serves 6

For the pastry:
1¼ cups (150g) whole-wheat flour
1¼ cups (150g) all-purpose flour, plus extra for dusting
½ cup plus 5 tbsp (200g) cold salted butter, cubed
1 tbsp sugar
splash of ice-cold water
1 egg, lightly beaten

For the filling:
roughly 10 plums
1 tbsp sugar, plus extra for sprinkling
juice and finely grated zest of 1 lemon
2 tbsp apricot jam
good pinch of chile flakes
handful of sliced almonds

YOU WILL NEED
large baking sheet, roughly 15 x 10½ in (38 x 27 cm), greased and lined with parchment paper

1. To make the pastry, place both types of flour and the butter into a large bowl and rub together with your fingertips until the mixture resembles breadcrumbs. Stir in the sugar, then add a splash or two of ice-cold water. Using one hand, shaped like a claw, mix everything together into a ball of dough, adding more water if needed. Flatten the dough into a disk, then wrap it in plastic wrap and chill for 30 minutes.

2. While the pastry is chilling, halve and stone the plums, then cut them into slices. Place the plums in a bowl, then stir in the sugar, lemon juice, and zest.

3. Preheat the oven to 350°F (180°C).

4. Generously dust your work surface with flour and roll out the pastry to roughly the same size as the lined baking sheet. I like an oval shape, but this is a rustic tart so don't worry too much about uniformity. Carefully lift the pastry onto the tray.

5. Spread the jam evenly over the pastry, then scatter over the chile flakes and top with the plums (you can go for uniform rows or just pile them on, it's totally up to you), leaving a 2 in (5 cm) border around the edge. Fold the edge of the pastry over the plum filling, gathering it where needed to make an open-topped oval tart.

6. Brush the edges of the pastry with egg, then sprinkle with sliced almonds and a little sugar. Bake for 35–45 minutes, until the pastry is golden and crisp, and the plums have softened. Let cool for 5 minutes or so on the baking sheet, then serve cut into slices.

Upside Down Crumble Tart

It just so happens that The Viking and I share the same birthday. On the surface, this sounds like a joyous thing, a double celebration, fun for all, but no, he is not a birthday fan. I have tried to make him fall in love with "our" day, and over the years, I think I've softened him to enjoy it more, and I've done this through food. This year, I asked him what his favorite type of birthday cake would be, and he said "peach or nectarine crumble." So, here it is in tart form...

Serves 6

For the pastry:
2 premade 9¾ x 10½ in
  sheets of puff pastry or use
  homemade (see p12) rolled
  to 14 x 9 in (35 x 23 cm)
2 tbsp chocolate spread
drizzle of honey
2 tbsp sugar
1 egg, lightly beaten

For the crumble:
⅓ cup (50g) all-purpose flour
¼ cup (30g) old-fashioned
  rolled oats
1¾oz (50g) sugar
3 tbsp (50g) cold butter, cubed

For the cake:
½ cup (60g) all-purpose flour
½ tsp baking powder
¼ tsp salt
4 tbsp (60g) salted butter,
  softened, cut into cubes
⅓ cup (60g) sugar
1 large egg
splash of whole milk
½ tsp vanilla extract
1 large ripe peach or nectarine,
  stone removed, flesh chopped

YOU WILL NEED
large baking sheet, roughly
  15 x 10½ in (38 x 27 cm),
  lined with parchment paper
8½ in (22 cm) diameter
  round plate

1 Preheat the oven to 425°F (220°C). Unroll the pastry and cut out an 8½ in (22 cm) round using the plate as a template. Spread the chocolate spread over one side of the pastry and fold it in half. Gently roll the pastry out again into a round slightly larger than the 8½ in (22 cm) round plate. Place in the fridge until needed.

2 Draw around the plate onto the parchment paper and place the paper drawn-side down on the baking sheet. Drizzle over a little honey and sprinkle with the sugar.

3 To make the crumble, using your fingertips, rub all the ingredients together in a bowl until they come together in large clumps—you don't want the mixture to be too fine. Set aside.

4 Whisk all the cake ingredients (apart from the fruit) in a large bowl using an electric hand whisk until light and creamy. This should take roughly 5 minutes.

5 With a spoon, dot some of the crumble mix randomly over the drawn circle on the lined baking sheet, then add a few spoonfuls of the cake batter and a scattering of peach or nectarine. Continue to build the cake in layers of crumble, cake batter, and fruit, then use your hands to gently press the mixture into a rough dome shape as you build.

6 Lay the pastry over the pile of crumble, cake, and fruit. Using the back of a teaspoon, scallop the edge to seal. Score the top in a diamond pattern with a sharp knife and then brush with egg.

7 Bake for 30 minutes, or until the pastry is golden and the cake is risen and firm. Remove the tart from the oven and let it sit on a wire rack for 5 minutes. Lay a piece of parchment paper and a cutting board or cake stand on top and flip it over. Remove the baking sheet and peel off the backing paper to reveal the tart. Serve cut into slices.

Spider's Web Upside Down Fruit Tart

Halloween is such a fun festival for kids and adults alike. While I adore Christmas treats, you can get away with being more creative at Halloween, combining spooky with tasty in one dish. This tart has both—the wow factor with its spidery decoration and blood-red berry and apple filling, and it also tastes fantastic.

Serves 6–8

4 premade 9¾ x 10½ in
    sheets of puff pastry or
    use homemade (see p12)
    rolled to two 14 x 9 in
    (35 x 23 cm) sheets
5 tbsp (75g) salted butter,
    softened
1 tbsp sugar
2 Granny Smith apples,
    peeled, cored, and cut
    into small cubes
3 tbsp mixed frozen berries
1 egg, lightly beaten

For the spider:
2 tbsp lemon curd
2 frozen blueberries for eyes

YOU WILL NEED
2 large baking sheets, roughly
    15 x 10½ in (38 x 27 cm),
    lined with parchment paper
4 in (10 cm) fluted cookie cutter
piping bag with small nozzle

1   Preheat the oven to 425°F (220°C). Unroll half the pastry, placing it vertically in front of you. Cut the pastry into ½ in (1 cm) wide strips, then place them on a baking sheet in the fridge until needed.

2   Smear the butter all over the lined baking sheet and sprinkle with the sugar. Arrange the pastry strips in a spider's web pattern on the lined tray (see pic, left).

3   Place the apples in a bowl and mix in the berries, then gently tip the mixture on top of the pastry spider's web in a rough rectangular heap in the middle, leaving a ¾ in (2 cm) border.

4   Unroll the remaining pastry, cut off a 4 in (10 cm) wide strip from one of the short ends to make the spider, then set aside in the fridge. Drape the larger piece of pastry over the apple mixture and trim the edges to neaten. Using the back of a fork, press around the edge of the pastry to seal. Score the top in a diamond pattern with a sharp knife and then brush with egg, leaving some to glaze the spider.

5   Bake for 30–35 minutes, until the pastry is golden and crisp. Remove the tart from the oven and let it sit on the baking sheet for 5 minutes. Lay a piece of parchment paper on top, followed by a cutting board, and carefully flip the tart over. Remove the baking sheet and lift off the backing paper.

6   While the tart is baking, make the spider. Using the cookie cutter, stamp out a disk of puff pastry for the body and cut 8 thin strips for the legs. Twist and bend the pastry legs and place on a second lined baking sheet with the spider's body. Brush with egg and bake for about 15 minutes, or until golden and puffed up. Let cool on a wire rack. Spoon the lemon curd into the piping bag. Make a hole in the side of the spider's body, insert the piping bag and squeeze in the curd. Carefully make four holes down each side of the body and insert the legs. Pipe small blobs of the lemon curd to make two eyes and top with the berries. Place the spider on top of the tart to serve.

Pumpkin Upside Down Pie

When I reached the sixth form (the last two years of senior school or high school), the boys in my year started to mix socially with girls from the school across the road, for obvious reasons. Clearly, those reasons didn't interest me, but to have some girl friends was heaven. This is when I met Shannon, who is still my friend today. Her family was American, and they introduced me to pumpkin pie. This is my tribute to her.

Serves 6

2 premade 9¾ x 10½in
   sheets of puff pastry or use
   homemade (see p12) rolled
   to 14 x 9in (35 x 23 cm)
1 recipe quantity of Shortcrust
   Pie Dough (see p12) rolled to
   roughly 14 x 9in (35 x 23 cm)
sprinkle each of ground
   cinnamon and sugar
drizzle of honey
1 tbsp demerara sugar
1 egg, lightly beaten

For the pie filling:
3 eggs
¾ cup plus 2 tbsp (175g) sugar
1 tsp pumpkin pie spice
1 cup (200g) canned pumpkin
   purée
⅓ cup (100ml) heavy cream
1 tsp ground cinnamon
½ tsp ground ginger
whipped cream, to serve

YOU WILL NEED
large baking sheet, roughly
   15 x 10½in (38 x 27 cm),
   lined with parchment paper
8in (20 cm) diameter
   round plate
leaf-shaped pastry cutters

1. Preheat the oven to 400°F (200°C). Unroll the pastry. Cut out an 8in (20 cm) round of puff pastry using the plate as a template. Sprinkle a light dusting of cinnamon and sugar over the puff pastry round and the shortcrust sheet. Put the puff pastry in the fridge until needed. Using the leaf-shaped cutters or a sharp knife, cut out as many leaves as possible using the shortcrust pastry—I like to use two different sizes of leaf. Place them on a tray in the fridge.

2. To make the pie filling, beat the eggs and sugar in a large bowl with an electric hand whisk until light and fluffy. Whisk in half of the mixed spice with the rest of the filling ingredients until combined. Set aside.

3. Draw around the plate onto the parchment paper and place the paper drawn-side down on the baking sheet. Drizzle over a little honey, then sprinkle with the remaining mixed spice and the demerara sugar. Brush a thick line of beaten egg around the marked line and arrange the pastry leaves on top. I like to place the leaves in a random pattern, overlapping them to form a circular wreath border. Repeat to make a double layer of leaves, and a barrier to hold in the pie filling. Brush the leaves with some of the beaten egg.

4. Pour in the pie filling, then drape the disk of puff pastry over the top. Using the back of a fork, press around the edge of the pastry to seal it to the decorative leaf border. Score the top in a diamond pattern with a sharp knife and then brush with egg.

5. Bake for 35–40 minutes, until the pastry is golden and crisp. Remove the pie from the oven and let it sit for at least 1 hour to cool and set. Lay a piece of parchment paper on top, followed by a cutting board or serving platter, and carefully flip it over. Remove the baking sheet and peel off the backing paper. Serve the pie cut into slices with heavy cream.

chris
time

.mas-

For a nice Jewish boy from north London, Christmas holds a special place in my heart. I guess it's because we didn't really celebrate it when I was a kid. Don't get me wrong, Father Christmas always came, and we would often visit relatives for the big-day meal, but we never put up a tree or decorations. It was just one day, then over. Now I'm grown up with my own home, we go big. The first day of December is the start for us. A real tree goes up, there are decorations everywhere, and the feasting begins. After all, I need little excuse to celebrate. And it's not just Christmas Day. There are myriad occasions to feast: from impromptu December gatherings to Boxing Day celebrations, and beyond to New Year's Eve. This chapter is a collection of festive meals and party treats to cater for everyone, from large get-togethers to more intimate soirees.

Caramelized Onion, Stuffing & Veggie Roast Christmas Pudding

The Viking says the worst thing about being a vegetarian is Christmas lunch. He's happy with just the vegetables and all the trimmings, but if I really want to go to town, I make this beauty, inspired by a recipe by the great Nigel Slater a few years ago. It's a savory pudding that takes the flavors of Christmas and layers them in a vegetable suet pastry case with delicious results. Serve it with your favorite Christmas sides and trimmings—and veggie gravy, of course!

Serves 6

For the filling:

3 tbsp (50g) butter
1 tbsp olive oil
4 large onions, finely sliced
1 tsp chopped rosemary leaves
1 tsp thyme leaves
7oz (200g) vegetarian roast
  from tofurkey or other
  meat-free protein
6oz (175g) sage and onion
  stuffing mix
salt and freshly ground
  black pepper

For the pastry:

2⅓ cups (300g) all-purpose
  flour, plus extra for dusting
2 tsp baking powder
1 tsp salt
¾ cup (150g) vegetable
  shortening
1 tsp chopped rosemary leaves
1 tsp chopped thyme leaves
scant 1 cup (200ml) ice-cold
  water

YOU WILL NEED

large heatproof glass or metal
  bowl, greased generously
  with butter

1 First, caramelize the onions. Heat the butter and olive oil in a large skillet on medium heat. Add the onions and cook gently for 30 minutes, stirring every 10 minutes or so (you may need to turn the heat down slightly to prevent them burning and sticking to the bottom of the pan), until caramelized. Add the herbs and cook for a further minute, stirring occasionally. Season with salt and pepper to taste, then set aside to cool.

2 Meanwhile, cook the vegetarian roast according to the package instructions, then cut it into roughly 12 thick slices. Make the stuffing mix following the package instructions. Set aside.

3 To make the pastry, in a large bowl, mix the flour, baking powder, salt, vegetable shortening, herbs, water, and a pinch of salt together to form a soft ball of dough. On a lightly floured work surface, roll out the dough until roughly ¼ in (5 mm) thick. Set aside enough pastry to make the lid, using the top of the bowl as a template, then use the remaining pastry to line the well-greased pudding bowl.

4 Begin to assemble the pudding, alternating between layers of caramelized onions, slices of veggie roast (you may need to trim them), and stuffing until the filling almost reaches the top of the bowl. Brush the edge of the pastry with water, then place the pastry lid on top and press the edges together to seal.

5 Cover the top of the bowl with a round of parchment paper and then foil, making a pleat down the middle of both to allow the pudding to expand, then secure with string. Place the bowl in a water bath and cook for 1 hour, adding more water, if needed.

6 Carefully remove the bowl from the pan and let it sit for 10 minutes, then remove the foil and paper. Slice the pudding into wedges and serve with the Christmas trimmings.

Upside Down Sausage, Brie & Cranberry Tart

If you're looking for an alternative to roast turkey, this tart makes a wonderful, all-in-one option for the big day. Combining classic festive ingredients, this simple recipe can be adapted to suit different tastes by adding your favorite herbs, spices, and other flavorings to the sausage meat. This version, however, is a good starting point and comes with my upside-down twist. It's one the whole family will love!

Serves 4–6

2 premade 9¾ x 10½ in sheets of puff pastry or use homemade (see p12) rolled to 14 x 9 in (35 x 23 cm)
6oz (175g) package of stuffing mix (I like sage and onion)
drizzle of olive oil
1 tsp chopped rosemary leaves, plus extra to garnish
1 tsp chopped thyme leaves
5½oz (150g) sausage meat
3½oz (100g) Brie cheese, cut into thick slices
2 tbsp cranberry sauce
1 egg, lightly beaten
salt and freshly ground black pepper

YOU WILL NEED
large baking sheet, roughly 15 x 10½ in (38 x 27 cm), lined with parchment paper

1 Preheat the oven to 425°F (220°C). Unroll the pastry and set aside.

2 Make the stuffing mix according to the instructions on the packet—I like to add a drizzle of olive oil to mine. Let cool.

3 Leaving a ½ in (1 cm) border, spread the stuffing mix over the pastry, then place in the fridge until needed.

4 Mark out a large rectangle on the parchment paper, the same size as the pastry, and place it drawn-side down on the baking sheet. Drizzle olive oil over the lined baking sheet, then sprinkle with the rosemary and thyme. Season with salt and pepper.

5 Leaving a ¾ in (2 cm) border, press the sausage meat in an even layer over the drawn rectangle. Lay the slices of Brie cheese over the sausage meat and dot spoonfuls of the cranberry sauce on top.

6 Carefully drape the pastry sheet, stuffing-side down, over the Brie cheese and sausage mixture. Using the back of a teaspoon, scallop the edges of the pastry to seal. Score the top in a diamond pattern with a sharp knife and then brush with egg.

7 Bake for 30–35 minutes, until the pastry is golden and crisp. Remove the tart from the oven and let it sit on the baking sheet for 5 minutes. Lay a piece of parchment paper on top, followed by a cutting board, then flip the tart over. Remove the baking sheet and peel off the backing paper to serve.

Upside Down Camembert & Chile Jam Snowflake

Is there anything more decadent and luscious than hot, melted Camembert cheese baked in a golden puff pastry case? The combination screams Christmas to me, and this tear-and-share treat is perfect for festive parties or as a starter on the big day itself.

Serves 4–6

4 premade 9¾ x 10½ in
  sheets of puff pastry or
  use homemade (see p12)
  rolled to two 14 x 9in
  (35 x 23 cm) sheets
3 tbsp chile jam (or mix
  half-and-half with Red Onion
  Jam, see p15)
drizzle of olive oil
1 tsp thyme leaves
9oz (250g) whole Camembert
  cheese, packaging removed
1 egg, lightly beaten
salt and freshly ground
  black pepper

YOU WILL NEED
large baking sheet, roughly
  15 x 10½ in (38 x 27 cm),
  lined with parchment paper
8½ in (22 cm) diameter
  round plate

1 Preheat the oven to 425°F (220°C). Unroll the pastry and cut out 2 large rounds using the 8½ in (22 cm) plate as a template. Using a rolling pin, roll out the pastry rounds to make them ¾ in (2 cm) larger in diameter. Spread the chile jam over one side of one of the pastry rounds and lay the second round of pastry on top. Place in the fridge until needed.

2 Drizzle olive oil over the lined baking sheet and sprinkle with the thyme. Season with salt and pepper. Place the Camembert cheese in the middle of the baking sheet and drape the pastry sandwich over the top. Press the sides of the pastry down to encase the cheese and form a pastry "skirt."

3 Make 12 evenly spaced cuts around the pastry "skirt," each one running from the cheese to the edge of the pastry. Take 2 strips of the pastry and twist them together, pressing the ends together in a point. Continue with the remaining strips of pastry to form 6 points. Score the top of the pastry in a diamond pattern with a sharp knife and then brush with egg.

4 Bake for 30–35 minutes, until the pastry is golden and crisp. Remove the pastry snowflake from the oven and let it sit on the baking sheet for 5 minutes. Lay a piece of parchment paper on top, followed by a cutting board, then flip the whole thing over. Remove the baking sheet and peel off the backing paper.

5 To serve, make a hole in the middle of the Camembert cheese, then break off the points of the snowflake to dunk into the melted cheese filling.

Upside Down Parsnip, Honey & Thyme Tarts

If you're anything like me, parsnips rarely get a look-in (apart from a spicy parsnip soup, perhaps, which I only make if I've bought too many parsnips for Christmas). I know the vegetable can be divisive, but I can assure you, this slightly sweet and fragrant tart, with a sharp hit from the grainy mustard, will make you question why you don't eat parsnips more often. This tart makes a great side dish or a vegetarian main course.

Serves 2–4

2 premade 9¾ x 10½ in sheets of puff pastry or use homemade (see p12) rolled to 14 x 9 in (35 x 23 cm)
2 tbsp whole grain mustard
drizzle of olive oil
1 tsp thyme leaves, plus extra to garnish
2 tbsp honey
4 parsnips, peeled, trimmed, and halved lengthwise
3½oz (100g) Gruyère cheese, grated
1 egg, lightly beaten
salt and freshly ground black pepper

YOU WILL NEED
large baking sheet, roughly 15 x 10½ in (38 x 27 cm), lined with parchment paper

1 Preheat the oven to 425°F (220°C). Unroll the pastry and cut it into 2 rectangles, each about 6½ x 9 in (17 x 23 cm). Spread 1 tablespoon of the mustard over each rectangle, leaving a narrow border. Place in the fridge until needed.

2 Mark out 2 rectangles on the parchment paper, the same size as the pastry and with space between each one, and place drawn-side down on the baking sheet. Drizzle olive oil over the lined baking sheet and sprinkle with the thyme. Season with salt and pepper, then drizzle over the honey.

3 Leaving a ¾ in (2 cm) border, arrange the parsnips on top of each drawn rectangle—I use 4 parsnip halves per tart, placed cut-side down. Scatter the Gruyère cheese over the parsnips.

4 Drape a pastry rectangle, mustard-side down, over each pile of parsnips. Using the back of a teaspoon, scallop the edges of each tart to seal. Score the tops in a diamond pattern with a sharp knife and then brush with egg.

5 Bake for 30–35 minutes, until the pastry is golden and crisp. Remove the tarts from the oven and let them sit on the baking sheet for 5 minutes. Lay a piece of parchment paper on top, followed by a cutting board, and carefully flip the tarts over. Remove the baking sheet and peel off the backing paper. Serve warm sprinkled with thyme.

Upside Down Brussels Sprout & Prosciutto Puffs

If you need to produce canapés at a moment's notice during the festive period, these little beauties use pantry ingredients and the humble, and much maligned, Brussels sprout, turning them into well-dressed puffs of festive joy.

Makes 12

2 premade 9¾ x 10½ in
  sheets of puff pastry or use
  homemade (see p12) rolled
  to 14 x 9 in (35 x 23 cm)
6 tsp cranberry sauce or jelly
drizzle of olive oil
drizzle of balsamic vinegar
1 cup (100g) Parmesan cheese,
  finely grated
6 Brussels sprouts, halved
  lengthwise
4 slices of prosciutto, each
  slice cut into 3 pieces
1 egg, lightly beaten
salt and freshly ground
  black pepper

YOU WILL NEED
large baking sheet, roughly
  15 x 10½ in (38 x 27 cm),
  lined with parchment paper
2¾ in (7 cm) plain cookie cutter
  or ramekin

1 Preheat the oven to 425°F (220°C). Unroll the pastry and, using the cookie cutter, stamp out 12 rounds. Spread ½ teaspoon of cranberry sauce in the middle of each round, leaving a narrow border. Place them on a baking sheet in the fridge until needed.

2 Using the same cookie cutter as a template, draw 12 disks (4 disks across and 3 deep) evenly spaced apart on the sheet of parchment paper. Place the paper drawn-side down on the baking sheet. Drizzle olive oil over the lined baking sheet and add a few splashes of balsamic vinegar. Season with salt and pepper.

3 Sprinkle the Parmesan cheese evenly over the drawn rounds. Place half a sprout, cut-side down, in the middle of each one and lay a piece of prosciutto on top.

4 Place the pastry rounds, cranberry sauce-side down, over each sprout. Using the back of a teaspoon, scallop the edges of each one to seal. Score a cross on top of the puffs with a sharp knife and then brush with egg.

5 Bake for 25 minutes, until the pastry is golden and crisp. Remove the puffs from the oven and let them sit on the baking sheet for 5 minutes, then slide a palette knife under each one to flip over before serving.

Upside Down Christmas Leftovers Quiche

In my first book, *"Upside Down Cooking,"* I created the Leftover Christmas Pie, which was a delicious way of using up any surplus roast turkey, vegetables, and stuffing left over from lunch. Well, here's its worthy successor... this tart has since become legendary in our home.

Serves 4–6

2 premade 9¾ x 10½ in sheets of puff pastry or use homemade (see p12) rolled to 14 x 9 in (35 x 23 cm)
about 14oz (400g) mix of Christmas leftovers, including turkey, roast potatoes, mashed potatoes, and stuffing, roughly chopped
3 eggs, lightly beaten
1 tbsp heavy cream
1¾oz (50g) feta cheese
1¾oz (50g) Cheddar cheese, finely grated
drizzle of olive oil
salt and freshly ground black pepper
gravy, for dunking (optional)

YOU WILL NEED
large baking sheet, roughly 15 x 10½ in (38 x 27 cm), lined with parchment paper

1 Preheat the oven to 425°F (220°C). Unroll the pastry and set it aside.

2 Tip the Christmas leftovers into a large bowl and pour over the beaten egg and cream. Add the feta and Cheddar cheese and stir well—the mixture should start to come together into a rough ball.

3 Mark out a large rectangle on the parchment paper, the same size as the pastry, and place it drawn-side down on the baking sheet. Drizzle over a little olive oil and season with salt and pepper.

4 Leaving a ¾ in (2 cm) border, spoon the Christmas quiche mixture on top of the drawn rectangle in an even layer.

5 Carefully drape the pastry over the quiche mixture. Using the back of a fork, press down the edges of the pastry to seal. Score the top in a diamond pattern with a sharp knife and then brush with egg.

6 Bake for 25–35 minutes, until the pastry is golden and crisp. Remove the tart from the oven and let it sit on the baking sheet for 5 minutes. Place a piece of parchment paper on top, followed by a cutting board, and flip the tart over. Remove the baking sheet and peel off the backing paper. Serve the slices of quiche with gravy for dunking.

Upside Down Mince Pie

This pie has become my go-to alternative to individual mince pies. You can make your own mincemeat but I always use premade, then add flavorings, such as orange and sometimes brandy. However, I always make my extra-special Christmas cream cheese and almond pastry. It's the best!

Serves 12

For the pastry:
1⅓ cup (300g) all-purpose flour, plus extra for dusting
¾ tsp baking powder
1 cup (110g) sugar
½ cup plus 2 tbsp (150g) cold unsalted butter, cut into small cubes
5½oz (150g) full-fat cream cheese
¾ cup (75g) ground almonds
1 egg yolk
splash of whole milk (optional)

For the rest of the tart:
5 tbsp (75g) unsalted butter, softened
1 tbsp honey
finely grated zest of 1 orange
14oz (400g) premade mincemeat
1 egg, lightly beaten
powdered sugar, for dusting
hard sauce or cream, to serve

YOU WILL NEED
large baking sheet, roughly 15 x 10½in (38 x 27cm), lined with parchment paper

1   To make the pastry, sift the flour, baking powder, and sugar into a large bowl. Using your fingertips, rub the butter into the dry ingredients until the mixture resembles breadcrumbs. Add the cream cheese, ground almonds, and egg yolk. Using the flat blade of a dinner knife, mix everything together to make a dough—you may need to add a little milk to help it bind. Shape the dough into a ball, wrap in plastic wrap, and chill for at least 30 minutes. (The pastry can be made up to 24 hours in advance and kept in the fridge or frozen for 3 months.)

2   Dust the worktop with plenty of flour. (The pastry is very short and crumbly, so be generous with the flour and gentle when you roll, plus flour will help when weaving the pastry lattice.) Cut the pastry in half and then roll out each half into a 16 x 10in (40 x 25cm) rectangle. Place one half in the fridge until needed. Take the other rectangle and cut lengthwise into ¾in (2cm) wide strips. Set aside.

3   Preheat the oven to 425°F (220°C). To assemble the tart, smear the softened butter over the lined baking sheet. Drizzle over the honey and sprinkle with the orange zest.

4   Lay half of the pastry strips diagonally on the baking sheet, placing them about 1in (2.5cm) apart. Now weave the remaining pastry strips over and under the strips on the baking sheet, arranging them in a criss-cross pattern so it looks like a woven basket. Alternatively, for an easier option, place the remaining strips diagonally on top. Carefully spoon the mincemeat over.

5   Drape the remaining pastry rectangle over the mincemeat and trim the edges of the pie to neaten. Using the back of a spoon, scallop the edges of the pastry to seal. Score the top in a diamond pattern with a sharp knife and then brush with egg.

6   Bake for 30–35 minutes, until the pastry is golden and crisp. Remove the pie from the oven and let it sit on the baking sheet for 5 minutes. Lay a piece of parchment paper on top, followed by a cutting board, and carefully flip the pie over. Remove the board and peel off the backing paper. Let cool slightly, then dust with powdered sugar. Serve with hard sauce or cream.

Upside Down Clementine & Almond Cake

Every Christmas, I like to make a clementine cake based on one by the fabulous Nigella Lawson (the origins of which are attributed to the revered Claudia Roden and her classic orange and almond cake). It's always hugely popular, and it turns out that many people across the world have their own version of this cake too, some including chocolate or made with other citrus fruits. Here, I've given the cake my upside-down twist by adding a layer of orange-infused crumble at the bottom (which becomes the top when turned over), adding a wonderful crunchy dimension to the bake.

Serves 8

For the cake:
roughly 13oz (375g) clementines, oranges, or other citrus fruit
6 large eggs, lightly beaten
1 cup plus 2 tbsp (225g) granulated sugar
2⅔ cups (250g) ground almonds
1 tsp baking powder

For the crumble:
½ cup (100g) sugar
¼ cup (50g) demerara sugar
finely grated zest of 2 large oranges
½ cup plus 2 tbsp (150g) cold lightly salted butter, cut into small cubes
½ cup granola or old-fashioned rolled oats
1¼ cup (150g) all-purpose flour
½ cup (50g) ground almonds
whipped cream, to serve

YOU WILL NEED
8 in (20 cm) round springform cake pan, greased, base and sides lined with parchment paper

1   To start the cake, place the clementines in a saucepan and pour over enough water to cover. Bring the water to a boil and cook for 1½ hours, adding more water as necessary, until the clementines are very soft. Drain, discarding the cooking water, and let the clementines cool. Cut each clementine in half and remove any pips. Put the fruit into a food processor—skin and all—and blitz for roughly 2 minutes, until smooth.

2   Preheat the oven to 375°F (190°C).

3   Now make the crumble. Using your fingertips, rub both types of sugar and the orange zest together in a mixing bowl to release the essential oils into the sugar. Add the rest of the crumble ingredients and rub together with your fingertips until it forms a chunky, crumbly mixture. Tip the crumble into the base of the cake pan and press down with the back of a spoon into an even layer. Set aside.

4   Tip the puréed clementines into a large bowl with the rest of the cake ingredients and mix well to a batter. Pour the mixture into the cake pan, over the crumble base, and level the top with a palette knife. Bake for 1 hour, or until golden and a skewer inserted into the middle comes out clean. (Check the cake after 40 minutes and cover the top of the pan with foil if the cake is becoming too dark.)

5   Remove the cake from the oven, leave it in the pan, and place it on a wire rack to cool completely. Place a plate or cake stand on top of the pan and turn the cake over to release it from the pan. Remove the lining paper and serve cut into slices with whipped cream on the side.

Pear & Chocolate Upside Down Tart

This tart has everything I love about the indulgence of Christmas: a nutty, creamy frangipane; rich, intense chocolate; buttery, flaky puff pastry, and sweet, juicy pears. What could be more perfect for a Christmas dessert or celebratory tea?

Serves 6–8

2 premade 9¾ x 10½ in sheets of puff pastry or use homemade (see p12) rolled to 14 x 9 in (35 x 23 cm)
1 tbsp melted butter
drizzle of honey
1 tbsp demerara sugar
3 just-ripe pears, peeled, halved lengthwise, and cored, each half cut into 3 wedges
1¾oz (50g) dark chocolate, chopped
finely grated zest of ½ orange
1 egg, lightly beaten
powdered sugar, for dusting

For the frangipane:
½ cup (120g) salted butter, softened
⅔ cup (120g) sugar
2 large eggs, lightly beaten
1¼ cups (120g) ground almonds
3 drops of almond extract

YOU WILL NEED
large baking sheet, roughly 15 x 10½ in (38 x 27 cm), lined with parchment paper
8½ in (22 cm) diameter round plate

1 Preheat the oven to 425°F (220°C). Unroll the pastry and cut out a round using the 8½ in (22 cm) diameter plate as a template. Place the pastry in the fridge until needed.

2 Draw around the same plate onto the parchment paper and place it drawn-side down on the baking sheet. Set aside.

3 To make the frangipane, cream the butter and sugar in a large bowl using an electric hand whisk for 3 minutes, or until pale and fluffy. Add the eggs and half of the ground almonds, and beat again until combined. Mix in the almond extract and the remaining ground almonds, then set aside.

4 Brush the melted butter over the drawn round on the lined baking sheet, then drizzle with a little honey. Sprinkle over the demerara sugar.

5 Leaving a ¾ in (2 cm) border, arrange the pears in a flower shape within the circle. Spoon over the frangipane and carefully spread it out evenly over the pears to cover. Scatter the chocolate and orange zest over the top.

6 Drape the pastry round over the pear and frangipane mixture. Using the back of a fork, press the edge of the pastry to seal. Score the top in a diamond pattern with a sharp knife and then brush with egg.

7 Bake for 30 minutes, until the pastry is golden and crisp. Remove the tart from the oven and let it sit on the baking sheet for 10 minutes. Lay a piece of parchment paper on top, followed by a cutting board or plate, and carefully flip it over. Remove the baking sheet and peel off the backing paper. Dust the top of the tart with powdered sugar before serving.

Sticky Toffee Christmas Pudding

We're not really Christmas pudding people in our house. For me, Christmas lunch is all about the incredible main course, and I'm always too full to eat anything other than a few chocolates. That said, if I'm craving dessert, this upside-down sticky toffee pudding is it; it's light but still has those indulgent Christmas dessert vibes, thanks to the warming spices and dried fruit. Plus, it is served with loads of brandy toffee sauce.

Serves 6–8

For the pudding:
4½oz (125g) dates, pitted
   and finely chopped
1¾oz (50g) mixed dried fruit
   and candied peel
⅓ cup (100ml) brandy
5 tbsp (75g) butter, softened
2 tbsp (25g) light muscovado
   sugar
2 eggs, lightly beaten
1½ cups (185g) all-purpose
   flour
1½ tsp baking powder
¾ tsp salt
large pinch of ground nutmeg
   and allspice
½ tsp ground cinnamon
1½ tbsp whole milk

For the brandy toffee sauce:
4 tbsp light muscovado sugar
1 tbsp honey
1 tbsp light corn syrup
2 tbsp salted butter
5 tbsp heavy cream, plus
   extra to serve
1½ tbsp brandy

YOU WILL NEED
large heatproof bowl, greased
   generously with butter

1 Put the dates, mixed fruit, brandy, and ⅓ cup (100ml) water in a saucepan over low heat (or do this in a microwave). Bring to a gentle simmer and cook for about 5 minutes, until the fruit has softened. Let cool.

2 Meanwhile, make the brandy toffee sauce. Place the muscovado sugar, honey, corn syrup, and butter in a small saucepan. Bring to a simmer and cook for 5 minutes, until the sugar dissolves. Remove the pan from the heat and gently pour in the cream and brandy. Return the pan to low heat and cook for a further 2 minutes, stirring continuously, then set aside.

3 To make the pudding, using an electric hand whisk, cream the butter and sugar in a large bowl until light and fluffy. (You can also do this in a stand mixer.) Add the eggs, flour, baking powder, salt, and spices and beat again until combined. Fold in the softened fruit and its liquid, then stir in the milk.

4 Pour a quarter of the brandy toffee sauce into the base of the prepared bowl, then spoon in the pudding batter. Place a sheet of foil on top of a sheet of parchment paper (they should be large enough to cover the top of the bowl with some overhang), then make a pleat down the center of both. Cover the bowl, parchment paper–side down, and tie it securely under the lip of the bowl using kitchen string.

5 Transfer the bowl to a water bath, cover, and cook over low heat for 3 hours, checking the water level every so often and adding more water when needed. Remove the paper and foil cover, then place a plate over the top of the pudding and flip it upside down out of the bowl. Warm the remaining sauce, then pour it over the pudding before serving with cream.

Cock
&
Can

tails
apés

My friend, Lisa, knows how to host a party. For her, it's not just about the food and drinks, the people, or even the location, it's about the joy you bring to it all. Everything you serve should be filled with fun, flavor, and color, and that's the vibe I'm trying to bring in this chapter. Here, I've paired my favorite cocktails with small bites or canapés, incorporating flavors and styles that complement each other. That said, feel free to mix things up! Cocktails and canapés should make you think about parties and bringing people together to celebrate. Nothing should be too perfect, rather it should be an abundance of feasting joy.

Upside Down Shrimp Tostadas

The Viking and I had an incredible trip to Puerto Vallarta, Mexico, last spring. This spicy shrimp canapé is inspired by a meal enjoyed on the beach there at sunset. Serve the upside-down mini tarts with my Marmalade Margarita (see p196) for the ultimate indulgent sundowner.

Makes 6

For the shrimp tostadas:
1 recipe quantity of Shortcrust
    Pie Dough (see p12) rolled to
    roughly 14 x 9 in (35 x 23 cm)
2 tbsp chile jam
7 oz (200g) large raw shrimp,
    peeled and deveined
2 garlic cloves, crushed
2 tsp chipotle (fajita)
    seasoning mix
2 shallots, cut into rings
1 egg, lightly beaten
salt and freshly ground
    black pepper

For the grilled guacamole:
½ small red onion, sliced
2 fresh red chiles, halved
    lengthwise and seeded
2 avocados, peeled and sliced
2 tomatoes, cut in half
juice and grated zest of 2 limes
2 tbsp extra virgin olive oil,
    plus extra for drizzling
1 garlic clove, crushed
1 tsp chipotle (fajita)
    seasoning mix
1 handful of cilantro leaves

YOU WILL NEED
large baking sheet, roughly
    15 x 10½ in (38 x 27 cm),
    lined with parchment paper
3½ in (9 cm) cookie cutter

1 Preheat the oven to 425°F (220°C). Unroll the pastry and stamp out 6 rounds using the cookie cutter. Spread a teaspoon of chile jam over one side of each round, leaving a narrow border around the edge. Place on a tray in the fridge until needed.

2 To make the grilled guacamole, put the onion in a large bowl with the chiles, avocados, and tomatoes. Add half of the lime juice, half of the olive oil, the garlic, and the seasoning mix. Mix gently until combined. Place a grill pan on medium heat. Lay the onion, chiles, and tomatoes in the hot pan and grill until golden in places and softened slightly. Set aside to cool. When cool, roughly chop the grilled vegetables and avocado with some of the cilantro leaves; you can go as small or chunky as you like. Place the guacamole in a bowl and season with salt. Stir in the rest of the lime juice and zest, and drizzle over some more olive oil. Set aside in the fridge while you make the tostadas.

3 Place the shrimp in a large bowl with 1 tablespoon of olive oil, the garlic, and seasoning mix. Mix well and set aside.

4 Using the cutter as a template, draw 6 rounds onto the sheet of parchment paper, leaving space between each one, and place drawn-side down on the baking sheet. Drizzle olive oil over the lined baking sheet, then season with salt and pepper. Leaving a narrow border around the edge, scatter the shallot rings over each marked round. Top with the shrimp, roughly 3 per tart, and spoon over the flavored oil in the bowl.

5 Drape a pastry round, chile jam-side down, over each pile of shrimp. Using the back of a teaspoon, scallop the edge of each pastry round to seal. Score a cross on the top of the puffs with a sharp knife and then brush with egg.

6 Bake for 25 minutes, or until the pastry is golden and crisp. Remove the tostadas from the oven and let them sit on the tray for 5 minutes before flipping over. Top with the guacamole and cilantro, then serve with a Marmalade Margarita.

Antipasti Rolls

These are my new go-to canapés. The options for fillings are almost endless, but I'm showing you my favorite Italian-inspired one. You must trust the process here and work fast to roll up the pastry when it comes out of the oven. Even though they're utterly messy to eat, these divine bites are delicious, fun, and a little bit silly. A Lemon Cosmopolitan (see p199) is the perfect zingy partner.

Makes about 18

2 premade 9¾ x 10½in sheets of puff pastry or use homemade (see p12) rolled to 14 x 9in (35 x 23 cm)
drizzle of olive oil
1 tsp chopped rosemary
1 tsp chopped thyme
1 egg, lightly beaten
⅔ cup (150g) Pesto (see p15) or use a purchased alternative
12 slices of prosciutto crudo
9oz (250g) mozzarella, drained, torn, or sliced
1 large bunch (about 1 cup) basil leaves
salt and freshly ground black pepper

YOU WILL NEED
large baking sheet, roughly 15 x 10½in (38 x 27 cm), lined with parchment paper

1 Preheat the oven to 425°F (220°C). Unroll the pastry and set aside.

2 Drizzle olive oil over the lined baking sheet and sprinkle with the rosemary and thyme. Season with salt and pepper.

3 Place the pastry on the lined baking sheet. Score the top in a diamond pattern with a sharp knife and then brush with egg. Bake for 25 minutes, or until golden and crisp.

4 Meanwhile, prepare the rest of your ingredients so you're ready to go when the pastry comes out of the oven, as you need to build the rolls while it is still warm.

5 Once the pastry is cooked and still warm, carefully place the baking sheet on a flat surface and begin to layer the filling ingredients. Start by slathering the pastry all over with pesto, then top with a layer of prosciutto, then mozzarella, and finally the basil leaves. Season with salt and pepper, then cut the pastry in half horizontally (from long edge to long edge).

6 Deftly roll up one of the topped pastry sheets, starting from a short edge, until you have a large roll. Repeat with the second sheet, then cut both rolls into 1 in (2.5 cm) thick slices. Serve on a platter with a Lemon Cosmopolitan.

Roast Tomato, Garlic & Mozzarella Sharing Platter

This sharing plate of roasted garlic and tomato-topped toasts, with the addition of mozzarella and fresh basil, is one of the messiest things to eat, but if the truth be told, that adds to its appeal. Originated by my friend, Lisa, the platter makes a phenomenal dish at a party, barbecue, or picnic—everyone just dives in and gets messy with it—especially with a glass or two of my Roast Tomato Bloody Mary (see p199).

Serves 6–8

1½lb (675g) small vine tomatoes (try and find a mix of sizes and colors, if possible)
1 large garlic bulb
4 tbsp extra virgin olive oil, plus extra to drizzle
4 tbsp balsamic vinegar
1 tsp dried oregano
1 generous handful of basil leaves
salt and freshly ground black pepper

To serve:

1 long baguette or 4 ciabatta buns
8oz (225g) cherry tomatoes, cut in half
3 large balls of mozzarella, 4oz (125g) each, drained and torn into pieces

YOU WILL NEED

large roasting pan

1 Preheat the oven to 400°F (200°C). Place the small vine tomatoes in a large roasting pan. Break the garlic bulb apart and scatter the cloves (still in their skins) around the tomatoes. Spoon over the olive oil and balsamic vinegar. Season with oregano, salt, and pepper, then add the basil leaves (saving some to serve). Roast in the oven for roughly 30 minutes, until the tomatoes are soft and beginning to burst, and the garlic cloves are tender. Turn off the heat but leave the pan inside the oven to let the tomatoes cool slowly.

2 Thickly slice the bread and drizzle both sides with olive oil. Place a grill pan on high heat and grill the bread on both sides until crisp and slightly blackened in places. Arrange the bread on a large cutting board or platter.

3 Remove the cooled roasted garlic and tomatoes from the oven. Squeeze the garlic cloves out of their skins onto the grilled bread and spread it out with the back of a spoon. Lay the roasted tomatoes on top of the garlic and squish them down slightly with the back of the spoon.

4 To serve, scatter the fresh tomatoes and mozzarella over the toasts. Season with salt and pepper, then scatter over some basil leaves. Drizzle generously with extra olive oil. Serve with a Roast Tomato Bloody Mary.

Upside Down Cherry & Feta Bites

I love a little treat I can pop into my mouth while cooking or waiting for guests to arrive, or to enjoy with a cocktail. Not that I need an excuse to nibble on these sweet-but-savory little bites. The juiciness of the cherries works well with the savory, salty feta, and they are perfect bedfellows with my ridiculously drinkable Blender Amaretto Sour (see p196).

Makes 16

1 recipe quantity of Shortcrust
    Pie Dough (see p12) rolled to
    roughly 14 x 9 in (35 x 23 cm)
drizzle of olive oil
1 tsp chopped thyme leaves,
    plus extra to garnish
1 egg, lightly beaten

For the filling:
9oz (250g) cherries, pitted
1 zucchini, chopped
1 tbsp chopped dill
½ tbsp chopped mint leaves
7oz (200g) feta cheese,
    crumbled
1¾oz (50g) unsalted,
    shelled pistachios
1 egg
salt and freshly ground
    black pepper

YOU WILL NEED
large baking sheet, roughly
    15 x 10½ in (38 x 27 cm),
    lined with parchment paper
2¼ in (5.5 cm) cookie cutter

1 Preheat the oven to 425°F (220°C). Unroll the pastry and stamp out 16 rounds using the cookie cutter. Place on a baking sheet in the fridge until needed.

2 Place all the ingredients for the filling in a food processor (reserving 16 cherries and a third of the feta cheese for later) and blend to a rough paste. Season with salt and pepper, then set aside.

3 Drizzle olive oil over the lined baking sheet and sprinkle with thyme. Season with salt and pepper. Arrange 16 cherries (in 4 rows of 4), evenly spaced apart, on the lined baking sheet.

4 Remove the pastry disks from the fridge and spread a teaspoon of the filling over the top of each one, leaving a narrow border around the edge.

5 Drape a pastry round filling-side down over the cherries. Using the back of a fork, press around the edge of the pastry rounds to seal. Score a cross on top of each one with a sharp knife and then brush with egg.

6 Bake for 25 minutes, or until golden and crisp. Remove the tarts from the oven and let them sit on the tray for 5 minutes. Slide a spatula underneath each one and deftly flip them over onto a serving platter. Scatter over a little extra thyme and the reserved crumbled feta cheese. Serve with a Blender Amaretto Sour. Cin cin.

Upside Down Chile Chutney Cauliflower Tarts

Cauliflower is such a versatile vegetable. If cooked correctly, it holds its shape and texture, without turning mushy, which is great for these mini tarts. It also readily absorbs flavorings, such as this lime and chile chutney. Any flavor will work, so choose your favorite and have fun with it. The tarts are perfect with a glass or two of my Rumdelion cocktail (see p199).

Makes 6

2 premade 9¾ x 10½ in
  sheets of puff pastry or use
  homemade (see p12) rolled
  to 14 x 9 in (35 x 23 cm)
6 tsp lime and chile chutney
drizzle of chile oil
6 cauliflower florets
drizzle of olive oil
1 egg, lightly beaten
salt and freshly ground
  black pepper

YOU WILL NEED
large baking sheet, roughly
  15 x 10½ in (38 x 27 cm),
  lined with parchment paper

1   Preheat the oven to 425°F (220°C). Unroll the pastry and cut it into 6 even-sized squares, each about 4½ x 4½ in (11 x 11 cm). Spread 1 teaspoon of chutney over the middle of each square, leaving a wide border. Place on a tray in the fridge until needed.

2   Mark out 6 squares on the parchment paper, the same size as the pastry and with space between each one, then place the paper drawn-side down on the baking sheet. Drizzle with the chile oil, then season with salt and pepper. Place a cauliflower floret in the center of each square and drizzle over some olive oil.

3   Drape a square of pastry, chutney-side down, over each floret. Using the back of a teaspoon, scallop the edge of each pastry square to seal. Score the top of the tarts in a diamond pattern with a sharp knife and then brush with egg.

4   Bake for 25 minutes, until golden and crisp. Remove the tarts from the oven and let them sit on the baking sheet for 5 minutes. Carefully slide a spatula underneath each one and deftly flip them over onto a serving platter. Serve with The Rumdelion cocktail.

The Art of Making Cocktails

When it comes to making cocktails, it's all about simplicity, speed, and just a little drama.

Preparation is key, and while I think a jug suits certain cocktails (and you should definitely own one!), the spectacle of shaking a cocktail or two is always something special. To keep the cocktails flowing, I have a few simple tips, beginning with an absolute must: a cocktail station. I suggest stocking it with the following:

- Large ice bucket, always filled with ice (you can never have enough ice)
- Selection of cut citrus fruit (lime, lemon, and orange slices or wedges)
- Selection of large jugs and stirrers
- Collection of cocktail shakers (one is never enough)
- Selection of glassware: highballs, shorts, wine glasses, and Martini-style glasses
- Salt or sugar in saucers, to add to the rims of your cocktail glasses
- No straws (straws are for children and just get in the way)
- Large high-speed blender (that can cope with ice)
- A friend who is happy to be the cocktail waiter for the evening.

Cocktail Time

I adore making cocktails but they must be quick and simple as well as convey an air of sophistication. On the following pages, I have included a few of my favorites, which all partner beautifully with the canapés in this chapter. Before you start, I recommend you have the prepared ingredients to hand and measured out, and to keep the cocktails flowing, I suggest a few essentials kitchen items (see p194 for my full list).

Marmalade Margarita

MAKES 2 *(pictured on page 184)*

This is a cute little twist on the classic margarita, made with the last scrapings in the bottom of a marmalade jar. I make the cocktail in the jar, which helps to loosen the residual marmalade and adds to the flavor.

INGREDIENTS
juice and finely grated zest of ½ orange
large handful of sea salt
ice
2 tbsp marmalade (any kind will work)
⅓ cup (100ml) tequila
1¾oz (50ml) fresh lime juice
1¾oz (50ml) triple sec

YOU WILL NEED
marmalade jar (near empty) or cocktail shaker

1   To start, decorate the rims of 2 martini glasses. Squeeze the orange juice into a shallow bowl and put the grated orange zest in a saucer. Add the salt to the zest and mix until combined. Dip the rims of the glasses into the orange juice, then into the orange zest-salt mix until coated. Set aside.

2   Add some ice to the marmalade jar containing 2 tablespoons of marmalade. Pour in the tequila, lime juice, and triple sec, then close the lid and shake well. If you don't have a near-empty marmalade jar, then add the ingredients to a cocktail shaker along with 2 tablespoons of marmalade and shake. Pour into the prepared glasses and enjoy.

Blender Amaretto Sour

MAKES 4 *(pictured right)*

I adore a sour cocktail; it appeals to my love of anything sweet-sharp. I also like cherries and almonds, so think of this cocktail as a cherry Bakewell tart in a glass, which is just as heavenly, and slightly deadly, as it sounds.

INGREDIENTS
1¾ cup (400ml) Amaretto liqueur
juice of 4–6 lemons (you need 1 cup/240ml)
2 egg whites
12oz (350g) jar of (pitted) black cherries in kirsch or cocktail cherries
ice

YOU WILL NEED
high-speed blender (one that can cope with ice)

1   Put the amaretto, lemon juice, egg whites, and 3 tablespoons of the kirsch or liquid from the jar into a blender. Add 5 cherries and a handful of ice. Whizz on high speed until pale and frothy, and starting to increase in volume.

2   Pour the cocktail into rocks glasses or tumblers and decorate with a cherry to serve.

The Rumdelion

MAKES 1 *(pictured left)*

They say that out of necessity comes invention, and this fabulous cocktail was invented by my husband, The Viking, during the COVID pandemic of 2020, when going to a bar wasn't an option. For those unfamiliar with Dandelion and Burdock, it has a wonderful flavor, with hints of licorice and vanilla, but if you can't find it, the best alternative is root beer or Dr Pepper.

INGREDIENTS

ice
1¾oz (50ml) dark spiced rum
5½oz (150ml) dandelion and burdock–
 flavored soda

1 Fill a highball glass with ice. Add the rum and top up with the soda. Stir.

Lemon Cosmopolitan

MAKES 1 *(pictured on p187)*

Mum and I have many things in common—our love of cakes, fish and chips, and having a good laugh spring to mind—but one of the best things I share with her is our love of a cosmopolitan. It's our go-to drink at any bar or party. This is a lemony twist on my favorite. It's one for the shaker, but it's so easy it can be made on repeat.

INGREDIENTS

1½oz (45ml) lemon vodka
½oz (15ml) triple sec
1oz (30ml) cranberry juice
½oz (10ml) lime juice
ice

To serve

1¼ in (3 cm) strip of orange peel

YOU WILL NEED

cocktail shaker

1 Put all the ingredients into a cocktail shaker, shake, and strain into a cocktail glass. Hold the orange zest about 4 in (10 cm) above your cosmo and very carefully wave it over a lit match or lighter flame. Bend the outer edge of the zest in toward the flame to release the orange oils, then add to your cocktail.

Roast Tomato Bloody Mary

MAKES 6 *(pictured on p189)*

This takes a regular Bloody Mary to another level. As for its reputation for curing a hangover, I'm not entirely sure, I'd probably consider it just an excuse to enjoy a cocktail—it's certainly delicious.

INGREDIENTS

3 cups (750ml) tomato juice
1¼ cups (300ml) vodka
ice, lemon slices, celery sticks, and Tabasco,
 to finish

For the roasted tomatoes:

1¾lb (800g) vine cherry tomatoes
splash of balsamic vinegar
2 tbsp olive oil
1 tbsp Worcestershire sauce
1 tsp chile flakes
1 tsp celery salt
3 garlic cloves
1 lemon, cut into wedges
salt and freshly ground black pepper

YOU WILL NEED

large roasting pan
high-speed blender

1 Preheat the oven to 350°F (180°C). Place all the ingredients for the roasted tomatoes in a large roasting pan. Season and mix well. Roast for 30 minutes, until the tomatoes are soft, then remove from the oven and let cool.

2 Discard the lemon wedges, then tip everything into a blender. Blitz until smooth, then pour in the tomato juice and vodka, and blend again briefly. Pour into a pitcher, and add ice and lemon slices. Serve in highball glasses with more ice, a stick of celery, and a dash of Tabasco.

Index

About the Author

Dominic Franks is a food writer and home cook who takes inspiration from Delia Smith, his mum, his Jewish heritage, and his London upbringing. He lives in Lincolnshire with his husband, Andy, where he has been cooking and writing for his food blog *Dom in the Kitchen* since 2010. He writes for *Lincolnshire Life Magazine* and is regularly featured on *BBC Radio Lincolnshire* as their food expert.

You can follow Dom on Instagram at **@dominthekitchen** and find more of Dom's recipes at **dominthekitchen.com**

Acknowledgments

I'd like to dedicate this book to Kyra. If I didn't, she would probably stop talking to me, and I'm hoping this goes at least a small way to repairing her omission from my first book, *Upside Down Cooking*.

I feel unbelievably honored that the team at DK had the confidence and faith in me to commission a second book. I'd very much like to start by thanking them and for guiding me through the process so smoothly. I've enjoyed every minute of it, perhaps even more so than the first book as I've been able to step back and relish the process, rather than feel like a deer caught in the headlights as I sometimes did with my first one. I'd like to thank Cara, Lucy, and Tania for being so brilliant, plus Cora and Silvia, who did such a tremendous job marketing *Upside Down Cooking*. My editor, Nicola, just makes the whole process so easy and continues to understand my quirks.

To any budding cookbook writer out there, my main piece of advice would be to get yourself a literary agent like Liza. Thank you for always being there for me.

Thank you to Ellis Parrinder, Susanna Unsworth, and Max Robinson, my photographer, food stylist, and stylist, who helped me create the unique vision for this book and for always being willing to take it to the next step.

Thank you again to Pauline at Nordic Ware for always being so supportive and generous with the supply of their amazing baking sheets and cake pans.

Thank you to Mum and Eric, and Dad and Jette—double the family, double the inspiration. As well as being a confidant, Mum can always be relied on for a hand-me-down recipe and a little mum wisdom when trying out new recipes. Dad is a secret keeper of family memories and many of them involve food, so he's always great to rely on for a bit of cooking retrospection. While the initial trauma of parental divorce can sting, a few decades on, my parents' spouses (or bonus mum and dad as we call them) have also become a well of recipe inspiration, for which I am grateful.

I'd like to thank Lisa, who once again gives the best advice and reminds me regularly to breathe, take it all in, and enjoy the process.

And, of course, to all my friends, I promise I'll call you, once you call me to let me know you've purchased this book! I'd like to extend a special thanks to Jenny and Phillipa, who have been so supportive and allowed me to be frivolous while they work so hard.

Again, I want to thank all my wonderful social media family. Thanks for the follows, likes, shares, and comments. It's a community that I treasure with all my heart. Thank you to Dawny, who works tirelessly behind the scenes.

And finally, to my husband, best friend, and constant companion, Andy (The Viking). Thank you for being here by my side. You are my everything.

Publisher's Acknowledgments

DK would like to thank John Friend for proofreading and Lisa Footitt for providing the index.

DK LONDON

Editorial Director Cara Armstrong
Senior Editor Lucy Sienkowska
Americanizer Sharon Lucas
US Consultant Renee Wilmeth
US Executive Editor Lori Cates Hand
Design Manager Tania Gomes
DTP and Design Coordinator Heather Blagden
Production Editor Becky Fallowfield
Senior Production Controller Stephanie McConnell
Art Director Maxine Pedliham
Publishing Director Stephanie Jackson

Editorial Nicola Graimes
Design Amy Child
Design Development Studio Nic & Lou
Photography Ellis Parrinder
Food Styling Susanna Unsworth and Kristine Jakobsson
Prop Styling Max Robinson

First American Edition, 2026
Published in the United States by DK Publishing,
a division of Penguin Random House LLC
1745 Broadway, 20th Floor, New York, NY 10019

ISBN: 979-8-2171-3957-6

Printed and bound in China
www.dk.com

This book was made with Forest
Stewardship Council™ certified
paper—one small step in DK's
commitment to a sustainable future.
Learn more at
www.dk.com/uk/information/sustainability